CHRISTIAN ENCOUNTERS

JOHN
BUNYAN

CHRISTIAN ENCOUNTERS

JOHN
BUNYAN

KEVIN BELMONTE

THOMAS NELSON
Since 1798

NASHVILLE   DALLAS   MEXICO CITY   RIO DE JANEIRO

DEDICATION

To John Brown, whose painstaking research and reverent
erudition has placed all students of Bunyan in his debt;
to C. S. Lewis, whose recorded lecture on
The Pilgrim's Progress has been a guiding inspiration;
and to the memory of William Nigel Kerr, whose kind encouragement
of a young author meant so much, and still does.

Published in Nashville, Tennessee, by Thomas Nelson. Thomas Nelson is a registered
trademark of Thomas Nelson, Inc.

Published in association with Rosenbaum & Associates Literary Agency, Brentwood, Tennessee.

Thomas Nelson, Inc., titles may be purchased in bulk for educational, business, fund-raising, or
sales promotional use. For information, please e-mail SpecialMarkets@ThomasNelson.com.

Scripture quotations marked KJV are from the KING JAMES VERSION (public domain).

Scripture quotations marked NASB are from the NEW AMERICAN STANDARD BIBLE®.
© The Lockman Foundation 1960, 1962, 1963, 1968, 1971, 1972, 1973, 1975, 1977. Used by
permission.

Library of Congress Cataloging-in-Publication Data

Belmonte, Kevin Charles.
 John Bunyan / by Kevin Belmonte.
  p. cm.
 Includes bibliographical references.
 ISBN 978-1-59555-304-1
 1. Bunyan, John, 1628–1688. 2. Authors, English—Early modern, 1500-1700—Biography.
3. Puritans—England—Biography. I. Title.
 PR3331.B45 2010
 828'.407—dc22
 [B]   2009042915

Printed in the United States of America

10 11 12 13 HCI 6 5 4 3 2 1

CONTENTS

Preface   ix

Prologue: The Great Gathering   xii

1. Legacy and Memory   1
2. Times That Tried Men's Souls   4
3. A Parish in the Hundred   10
4. A Goodly Heritage   17
5. The Tinker of Elstow   21
6. "The Glad Reason of Life"   26
7. Scholarship of the Slenderest Kind   32
8. Disquieting Intimations   41
9. Rumors of War   46
10. A Nameless Love   51
11. The Unexpected Dowry   55
12. "A Path That Skirted Madness"   60
13. The Coming of Evangelist   69
14. A Mender of Souls   77
15. "No Ordinary Difficulties"   85
16. Prisoner of Conscience   91
17. "The Fortunate Limits of Imagination"   105
18. "Fancies That Lit the Prison Cell":   112
    The First Part of *The Pilgrim's Progress*

19. Bunyan's Immortal Story: 123
    The Second Part of *The Pilgrim's Progress*

20. "Great Extremes"   132

21. The House on Snow Hill   136

Epilogue: Relics   140

Appendix: A Bunyan Timeline   143

Notes   146

Select Bibliography   166

Acknowledgments   168

About the Author   171

It was an age of great revolutions, great excitement, great genius, great talent; great extremes both in good and evil; great piety and great wickedness; great freedom and great tyranny and oppression. Under Cromwell there was great liberty and prosperity; under the Charleses there was great oppression and disgrace. [John] Bunyan's life, continuing from 1628 to 1688, embraces the most revolutionary and stirring period in English history.

—George Barrell Cheever (1844)

There may be some—I do not know if there are— who will be so much alienated by the seventeenth century apparatus of the great story . . . so weary of old texts, so scornful of old doctrines, that they will fancy that this ancient Puritan poetry of danger is interesting only from a literary and not at all from a philosophical or religious point of view. For such people there is, I suppose, still waiting untried that inevitable mood in which a man may stand amid a field of flowers in the quiet sunlight and realise suddenly that of all conceivable things the most acutely dangerous thing is to be alive.

—G. K. Chesterton (1904)

PREFACE

Revere the man, whose PILGRIM marks the road,
And guides the PROGRESS of the soul to God.

—William Cowper

During my senior year of high school I was given an assignment: "Choose a classic text of English literature," we were told, "and write a research paper about it." The crisp temperatures of fall had come to southern New Hampshire; and outside the windows of my classroom, the trees displayed their autumn finery as I wrote about *The Pilgrim's Progress*. It was a highlight of my fourth-year Honors English class at Exeter High School. I learned how pervasive the influence of John Bunyan's allegory had been—how it had shaped the development of the English language—and the ways in which its simply wrought cadences had bequeathed phrases still quoted today: "the slough of Despond," "Vanity Fair," and "the man so bravely play'd the man, he made the fiend to fly." I read of vividly conceived characters like Greatheart, whose influence on the young Theodore Roosevelt (to cite but one example) was profound. I encountered imagery that has inspired writers from Thackeray to C. S. Lewis. The intervening years have only underscored that initial set of impressions and deepened my interest in what is, by any measure, a most remarkable work.

That the work and its author are remarkable has drawn many a memorable phrase from some of the best writers to put pen to paper over the last three hundred years. "Literature," wrote the literary adventurer and anthologist Thomas Budd Shaw in 1849, "presents no more original personality than that of John Bunyan, the greatest master of allegory that ever has existed."[1] Another and more celebrated Shaw—George Bernard Shaw—went one better, claiming that Bunyan excelled Shakespeare as a master of prose. No less a commentator than G. K. Chesterton, Shaw's friendly literary rival and celebrated debating opponent, observed:

> The writer whom [Shaw said] was better than Shakespeare was not himself, but Bunyan. And he justified it by attributing to Bunyan a virile acceptance of life as a high and harsh adventure, while in Shakespeare he saw nothing but profligate pessimism . . . According to this view, Shakespeare was always saying, "Out, out, brief candle" . . . while Bunyan was seeking to light such a candle as by God's grace should never be put out.[2]

The era in which Bunyan lived has been no less fecund in prompting its share of memorable reflections, such as this, written in 1844 by the literary critic and essayist George Barrell Cheever:

It was an age of great revolutions, great excitement, great genius, great talent; great extremes both in good and evil; great piety and great wickedness; great freedom and great tyranny and oppression. Under Cromwell there was great liberty and prosperity; under the Charleses there was great oppression and disgrace. Bunyan's life, continuing from 1628 to 1688, embraces the most revolutionary and stirring period in English history.[3]

Cheever's vivid description recalls the opening of *A Tale of Two Cities*, the Dickensian novel that it predates by some fifteen years. That Cheever was a writer of no mean skill is underscored by the fact that he was a member of one of the most famous graduating classes in American literature—the Bowdoin College Class of 1825—which counted among its members Nathaniel Hawthorne and Henry Wadsworth Longfellow.

Suffice it to say, there are many reasons why Bunyan's life makes for fascinating reading. But what of his great book? What about its story? How, and why, was *The Pilgrim's Progress* written? The search for answers to those questions gave rise to this book.

—Kevin Belmonte
Woodholme
April 2009

PROLOGUE

THE GREAT GATHERING

November 1928—let us say the thirtieth of November. The three-hundredth anniversary of John Bunyan's birth. It had been a year of literary celebrations, none more important than the banquet held on Wednesday, June 6, at the Goldsmith's Hall in London to mark the completion of the *Oxford English Dictionary* (the OED). The prime minister, Stanley Baldwin, was in attendance—as were 150 others (women not included)—"each one of whom was monumentally distinguished in achievement and standing."[1] Invitations to this august assemblage were highly prized and angled for, at times, in unseemly ways.[2] Everyone, it appeared, wanted to be there.

The OED is, of course, the greatest monument to English literature. But if individual works were singled out for inclusion in a pantheon of the greatest works in the language, Bunyan's masterwork, *The Pilgrim's Progress*, would surely be among them. And while the precise date of Bunyan's birth is unknown—November 30 is the date of his baptism in the parish church of Elstow—one cannot help wondering what it would have been like if a banquet of the kind held to honor the completion of the OED were to have taken place. Who would have been invited? And—if the constraints of time and place could have been suspended for an evening, who would have desired to be there?

For a start, the list would have included many women. Mary Ann Evans, better known as George Eliot, would be among them. Her novels were studded with references to Bunyan and his book—*Middlemarch* and *Adam Bede* to name but two. Her diary for November 25, 1859, offers this tribute, as representative as any she wrote: "I am reading old Bunyan again, after the long lapse of years, and am profoundly struck with the true genius manifested in the simple, vigorous, rhythmic style."[3]

Moving alphabetically to the top of the list, we would surely encounter Jane Austen, whose novels reflect Bunyan's influence in her use of landscapes to suggest spiritual themes. One can see this, for example, in various elements of *Mansfield Park*, such as the iron gate and winding woodland path.[4] Indeed, there are many ways in which *Mansfield Park* might be seen as Jane Austen's *Pilgrim's Progress*, with the characters Edmund and Fanny serving as the Christian hero and heroine.[5]

In 1852, Harriet Beecher Stowe published *Uncle Tom's Cabin*—her immortal antislavery version of *The Pilgrim's Progress*—.[6] That Bunyan's writings shaped her moral imagination is clear from a letter she wrote some years later, while in Switzerland and in sight of the Alps:

This morning we started early from Grindelwald . . . an unclouded, clear, breezy morning. . . . I said to [my companion]: "The more of beautiful scenery I see, the more I appreciate the wonderful poetry of *The Pilgrim's Progress*. The meadows by the River of Life, the Delectable Mountains, the land of Beulah, how often have I thought of them!"[7]

Closer to Bunyan's time, Samuel Johnson—"arguably the most distinguished man of letters in English history"[8]—would insist on being among the assembled guests. One can imagine words he wrote about Bunyan forming a toast he would offer in measured, stentorian tones: "Few books," the great Cham would aver, "have had a more extensive sale. [*The Pilgrim's Progress*] has great merit, both for invention, imagination, and the conduct of the story; and it has had the best evidence of its merit, the general and continued approbation of mankind."[9]

Crossing the ocean to America, Johnson's contemporary Benjamin Franklin might offer a memorable tribute of his own—one taken directly from the pages of his classic *Autobiography*: "From a child I was fond of reading, and all the little money that came into my hands was ever laid out in books. Pleased with *The Pilgrim's Progress*, my first collection was of John Bunyan's works in separate little volumes." Still later, Franklin praised Bunyan in an unlikely and rather inglorious setting: a recollection of his journey to Philadelphia as a young man seeking his fortune. Part of that trip involved a brief sail near Long Island in a small craft that was none too seaworthy. It was blown about and battered by a squall, during which time Franklin rescued a drunken Dutchman who fell overboard, reaching down through the water to his shock pate and drawing the hapless man up and back into the boat. Rather than thank Franklin profusely for saving his life, the Dutchman's only thought seemed to be for a book in his pocket that he kept asking Franklin to dry for him. He soon saw why: the book was a finely printed Dutch edition of *The Pilgrim's Progress*. It must have been expensive, and as he looked back on the incident, Franklin reflected:

> Honest John was the first that I know of who mix'd narration and dialogue; a method of writing very engaging to the reader, who in the most interesting parts finds himself, as it were, brought into the company and present at the discourse. Defoe in his *Crusoe*, his *Moll Flanders* . . . and other pieces, has imitated it with success; and Richardson has done the same, in his *Pamela*.

Returning to the nineteenth century, one immediately thinks of Charles Dickens's indebtedness to Bunyan, as expressed in *Oliver Twist*, subtitled *The Parish Boy's Progress*. Thackeray's debt to Bunyan is perhaps better known, the allegorical place-name of "Vanity Fair" supplying the title of his classic novel.

"I sing daily with my Bunyan, that great bard," Robert Louis Stevenson wrote to a friend from a sunlit garden one afternoon in May 1883. He followed this with an apposite quote: "I dwell already the next door to Heaven!"[10] In the same year, Stevenson had published his own epic tale, *Treasure Island*. He had, it seemed, always enjoyed Bunyan. He looked back upon "the pleasant maternal casuistry" of his childhood days "when a pack was sewn on to the back" of one of his wooden play figures and he had played "Pilgrim's Progress" all day.[11] As a young man he described the "wisdom and happiness" he had derived from his reading of Shakespeare, Dumas, and Bunyan.[12]

"Shakespeare has served me best," he wrote, "my dearest and best friend outside of Shakespeare is D'Artagnan . . . Lastly, I must name the *Pilgrim's Progress*, a book that breathes of every beautiful and valuable emotion." He would later repay his debt in a classic essay that has served as an introduction for many subsequent editions of *The Pilgrim's Progress*.[13]

For the thousands of American girls who so avidly read Louisa May Alcott's *Little Women* in the nineteenth century, Bunyan was "as familiar as toast and tea."[14] Alcott, like Stevenson, had played "Pilgrim's Progress" as a child. Drawing on those memories, she re-created those times of play with her sisters in the first chapter of *Little Women*.

> "Do you remember how you used to play *Pilgrim's Progress* when you were little things?" Mrs. March asked. "Nothing delighted you more than to have me tie my piece bags on your backs for burdens, give you hats and sticks and rolls of paper, and let you travel through the house from the cellar, which was the City of Destruction, up, up, to the housetop, where you had all the lovely things you could collect to make a Celestial City."
>
> "What fun it was, especially going by the lions, fighting Apollyon, and passing through the valley where the hob-goblins were," said Jo.
>
> "I liked the place where the bundles fell off and tumbled downstairs," said Meg.

Nathaniel Hawthorne, the literary lion whose writings evoked New England's Puritan past, was profoundly influenced by Bunyan.[15] "Hawthorne in his younger years," the novelist Henry James observed, "had been a great reader and devotee of Bunyan and Spenser."[16] Hawthorne's literary indebtedness to *The Pilgrim's Progress* was substantial. Indeed, it has long been recognized as a major source and inspiration for his art.[17]

One can see this most overtly in *The Celestial Railroad*, Hawthorne's industrial age–adaptation of *The Pilgrim's Progress*. But there are many echoes of Bunyan throughout his works, among them *The Scarlet Letter*, *The House of the Seven Gables*, and *The Blithedale Romance*.[18]

Still, it could be argued that the greatest literary debt to Bunyan in the nineteenth century is that owed by Mark Twain, whose *Adventures of Huckleberry Finn* (1884) was a quest of self-discovery set in the American South.[19]

The Pilgrim's Progress was a book of absorbing interest to Twain throughout the late 1880s—so much so, that it became the basis of one of his celebrated grand schemes. That in the end this scheme came to nothing takes little away from the significance Twain attached to Bunyan's work. It captured his fertile imagination and called forth the nineteenth-century equivalent of a lavish multimedia presentation—a Victorian-era surround-sound omni-theater spectacle. *The Pilgrim's Progress* done on a George Lucas/Steven Spielberg scale. Twain's biographer, Albert Bigelow Paine, recounted the story:

> [Twain] was deeply interested in *Pilgrim's Progress* . . . and from photography and scenic effect he presaged a possibility today realized in the moving picture. "Dress up some good actors," he recorded in his notebook, "as Apollyon,

Greatheart, etc., & the other Bunyan characters . . . and photograph them [in] Cairo, Venice, Jerusalem, & other places . . . It would take two or three years to do the photographing & cost $10,000; but this stereopticon panorama of Bunyan's *Pilgrim's Progress* could be exhibited in all countries at the same time & would clear a fortune in a year. By & by I will do this."[20]

This is the first recorded instance of anyone wishing to bring Bunyan's epic to the big screen. And it was Twain who conceived the project, envisioned its exotic set locations, and proposed to fund it. The audacity of the project is as striking as the thought of what such a stereopticon presentation would have looked and sounded like. Twain wanted to push the limits of existing technology to bring Bunyan to the masses. It was a grand vision, even if never realized.

Twain's younger contemporary, Theodore Roosevelt, would have added more than a little dash and color to a banquet honoring Bunyan.[21] It was he who assembled "America's most famous bookcase" when setting out for Africa in 1909. *The Pilgrim's Progress* was among the ruggedly bound volumes that comprised his "Pigskin Library"—books meant to withstand the rigors of an arduous trek and solace the hours of rest Roosevelt and his son Kermit took from the trail. This library, Roosevelt wrote, was comprised of many of "the books we most care for [and] thought we should like to take on this particular trip."[22]

The story has an interesting close. The list of books in the Pigskin Library (published in the book *African Game Trails*) ignited a spirited debate with C. W. Eliot, the president of Harvard, as to which books really were essential reading. It seems Eliot had just published his own list.[23]

Roosevelt died in 1919—the same year that marked the passing of L. Frank Baum, creator of *The Wizard of Oz*—one of the most beloved of all children's stories. The 1939 film adaptation of Baum's tale, starring Judy Garland, has itself become a masterpiece of cinema. For nearly three generations, parents and children have shared a bit of its magic together. Annual telecasts of film have become a fixture of the holidays—eagerly anticipated, cherished times when parents can become children once more alongside their own children.

Less well known is the extent to which Baum drew on *The Pilgrim's Progress* when crafting *The Wizard of Oz*. A considerable literature tracing the connections and similarities between the two stories has emerged.[24] Both are quest stories—Dorothy seeking the Emerald City, Christian the Celestial. Both tales unfold in the midst of a dream. A wilderness setting figures prominently in each, the wizard of Oz telling Dorothy that he, like her, was born in "the Western wilderness" of Kansas; while Bunyan commences *The Pilgrim's Progress* with one of the most famous first lines in all literature: "As I walked through the wilderness of this world, I lighted on a certain place where was a den, and laid me down in that place to sleep; and, as I slept, I dreamed a dream." There is even a witch to be found in Bunyan's story, Madam Bubble, who appears to pilgrims casting gold-like dust from her purse to tempt and lure them into bondage.[25]

Similarities between the two stories might be drawn *ad infinitum*; but perhaps the most satisfying thought of all is the idea that two such beloved stories bear so many points of connection with each other.

All pleasant imaginings of a celebratory banquet for Bunyan aside, or speculation about who might wish to be there, it is sufficient to say that one could fill a very stout book with stories of how a book written by a largely self-taught tinker—a mender of pots and kettles—shaped the development of English literature and Western culture. And this is the crux of the matter: how did such a great book come to be written by a man of such modest origins? The answers to that not insignificant question have given rise to the pages that follow.

①

LEGACY AND MEMORY

Genius knows no laws save its own, observes no
precedents, but wherever it occurs, it remains one
of the perennial human mysteries. John Bunyan in
his day personified that mystery.[1]

—Ola Winslow

Bedford, England, 1838. The ancient and celebrated
cottage on St. Cuthbert Street was to be demolished.
No historical commission intervened, and someone
surely should have, for the cottage had once been home to John
Bunyan, whose book *The Pilgrim's Progress* has earned an unas-
sailable place in the literary canon.

And so the home where Bunyan lived from 1655 until his
death passed into memory, its site now marked by one of the
ubiquitous blue plaques that dot the British landscape. No one
would ever again be able to ascend stairs upon which the great

man had walked, or look out from windows from which he had seen the wider world.

But the cottage, and Bunyan himself, had one final legacy to reveal: workers removing bricks from the cottage chimney discovered a Deed of Gift he had written and hidden in 1685, bequeathing his entire estate to his wife, Elizabeth. Twice imprisoned, he had been fearful that the authorities might arrest him yet again and seize his possessions. The discovery of this document meant that yet another of his legacies had transcended the years.

Of course, Bunyan's most transcendent legacy is a literary one. The imagery conjured by *The Pilgrim's Progress* fired the artistic vision of William Blake. Its themes led the composer Ralph Vaughan Williams to pen an opera. Writers from Thackeray to C. S. Lewis have drawn inspiration from the tinker whose simple cadences transformed the language. George Eliot, Samuel Johnson, Coleridge, and Macaulay—as well as presidents Lincoln and Roosevelt—have all acknowledged the greatness of *The Pilgrim's Progress*. It is, quite simply, one of the finest works in the English language.

Nor is the claim of Bunyan's book to immortality confined to the sanctions of the great—whether literary lions or leaders whose images grace the peak of Mount Rushmore. It was Macaulay who observed in an *Edinburgh Review* essay that many early editions of *The Pilgrim's Progress* were "evidently meant for the cottage and the servant's hall."[2] It was, then, very much a book for the common people.

Macaulay was not one to suffer fools gladly, and he did not hesitate to puncture pomposity, whether literary or cloistered within the halls of academe. In his essay, he took direct aim at both. "In general," he observed, "when the educated minority and the common people differ about the merit of a book, the opinion of the educated minority finally prevails. *The Pilgrim's Progress* is perhaps the only book about which, after the lapse of a hundred years, the educated minority has come over to the opinion of the common people."[3]

We can be grateful that Bunyan's book found an enduring place in cottages and servants' halls. Its availability in cheap editions ensured that the young Abraham Lincoln could absorb and distill its rhythms and style. Homes of the time, if they had any books, were most likely to have a copy of *The Pilgrim's Progress*. Echoes of the King James Bible, along with Bunyan's prose, influenced the spare and graceful cadences of the Gettysburg Address.[4]

The Pilgrim's Progress, apart from its considerable literary legacy, has a fascinating history—one only hinted at in what has been said above. And if ever a book were to have a biography written about it, Bunyan's book is most deserving of one.

2

TIMES THAT TRIED
MEN'S SOULS

There are, [I] think, some characters and scenes in *The
Pilgrim's Progress*, which can be fully comprehended
and enjoyed only by persons familiar with the history
of the times through which Bunyan lived.

—Thomas Babington (Lord Macaulay)

an is born unto trouble, as the sparks fly upward."
So we read in the book of Job (5:7 KJV). But these
words could well describe the world in which John
Bunyan lived. It was tumultuous and tragic by any measure.[1]
Wars and religious conflicts threatened to tear Britain apart, and
very nearly did.

In January 1649, when Bunyan was twenty, Charles I was
beheaded outside the palace of Whitehall. This regicide had been
preceded by two civil wars in four years, and it was followed by

the establishment of the Commonwealth of England. A republic had replaced the monarchy. On December 16, 1653, Oliver Cromwell became Lord Protector of Britain. He died in early September 1658, and was succeeded by his son Richard.

However, in the spring of 1659, Richard Cromwell was forced to resign. George Monck, now head of the army, briefly assumed power. Less than one year later, he was deposed when the monarchy was restored, and Charles II became king in May 1660.

This second Charles, as royal a rake as ever has been, had his revenge. In 1661, Oliver Cromwell's body was exhumed from Westminster Abbey, and on January 30, the same date Charles I had been executed, Cromwell's body suffered a posthumous execution. They beheaded him, threw his body into a pit, and displayed his severed head on a pole outside Westminster Abbey for the next twenty-four years. In what has to be one of the more macabre side notes of British history, Cromwell's head was treated as a ghastly souvenir, passing through several owners over the next century and a half. As late as 1814, it was sold to one Josiah Henry Wilkinson. Another 146 years would pass before Cromwell's remains found something like a final rest. His head was buried on the grounds of Sidney Sussex College, Cambridge, in 1960, almost three hundred years after being exhumed.

One regicide, two civil wars, five heads of government in twelve years. Sporadic outbreaks of religious persecution contingent on who was in power. Under the Commonwealth of Cromwell, Catholics in Ireland were treated brutally. Thousands were dispossessed of their lands during this violent regime. Cottages and houses were burnt, and their owners "cut down or hanged without mercy."[2] The Sack of Wexford and Siege of Drogheda became bywords for massacre and treachery. At Wexford, the garrison commander was trying to negotiate a surrender when parliamentary troops stormed in, killing soldiers and civilians alike. Thousands died.[3]

After the Commonwealth's demise, and under the reign of Charles II, conditions for dissenters were no less life threatening. During his trial in 1661, the presiding judge threatened Bunyan with perpetual banishment if he refused to "leave off preaching." Further, he was told that if he were to be banished, and "was again found in the country without special licence to return from the King, he would stretch by the neck for it."[4]

One year later, in 1662, the Act of Uniformity was passed. It was then, Roger Sharrock wrote, that "the full tide of persecution fell upon the dissenters."

> Hundreds of ministers who would not accept the Book of Common Prayer or Episcopal ordination were ejected from the [clerical positions] they held under the Commonwealth. In 1664 a new and more severe Conventicle Act was passed which prescribed crippling fines or imprisonment for [dissenters adjudged guilty]; the Five Mile Act of 1665 drive the ministers [from] city limits and outside their former [districts]. Not till the expiration of the Conventicle Act in 1668 . . . was there any relaxation of these measures.[5]

Like so many dissenters, Bunyan was in prison, where he would remain for twelve years. In a dirty, overcrowded cell, his blind daughter, Mary, visited, bringing the solace of food and soup for his supper in a stoneware jug now housed in the museum that bears his name.[6] Beyond the doors of the Bedford county gaol, ministers went into hiding.[7] Thousands of dissenters cherished their faith in secret, and many feared for their lives.

With good reason. For an extended period, beginning in May 1670, the government redoubled its efforts to put an end to all religious services outside the Church of England.[8] Local magistrates created a network of spies to hunt down and inform on people who took part in nonconformist religious gatherings. John Bunyan was already in prison, but his friends and loved ones were not, and when the district between Bedford and Cambridge was placed under surveillance, it put them in danger.

This nationwide system of espionage had been more or less at work ever since the passing of the Act of Uniformity in 1662; but in 1670–71, it became far more active. Spies earned handsome rewards for hunting down peaceable people. Once offenders were identified, the authorities reported their names to the central government where they were entered in a "Spy Book." People were never sure who to trust. By night, spies used stealth and infiltration to find out where dissenters were holding their meetings. By day, the spies hid in trees and combed forests to search out hidden places of meeting.

Other crises emerged. An outbreak of plague threw London into a panic in 1665. At its height, as many 6,000 died a week— perhaps as many as 100,000 in all. People were only just beginning to return to the city in 1666, when the Great Fire turned the skies into a scene from the apocalypse.

Seismic political shocks were far from over. In April 1685 James II was crowned king, succeeding his brother Charles, who died without leaving an heir.

However, Charles's illegitimate son, the Duke of Monmouth, wasn't about to countenance his uncle's accession to the throne. Rebellion broke out on two fronts, led by Monmouth in southern England and his ally, the Duke of Argyll, in Scotland.

Monmouth declared himself king; but forces loyal to James quickly quashed the rebellion. They captured Monmouth following the battle of Sedgemoor and beheaded him. Rebels who had sided with him were treated with extreme cruelty in a series of trials called the "Bloody Assizes." Judge Jeffreys, known as the "hanging judge," presided over the trials of thousands of these prisoners, ordering hundreds to be hanged immediately, and others to be hanged first, then drawn and quartered. Nor were the aged and infirm spared. The assize found one elderly gentlewoman, Dame Alice Lisle, guilty of treason and sentenced her to be burned at the stake. Here some mockery of mercy intervened, and the sentence was commuted to beheading.[9]

Nearly a thousand souls were transported by the government to the West Indies as slaves, deemed to be worth more alive than dead as a source of cheap labor. Many others who had been imprisoned in filth and squalor died of "gaol fever" or typhus.

The assize that took place in the Great Hall of Taunton Castle was representative. Of the more than 500 prisoners brought before the court in two days, 144 were hanged, and their bodies displayed throughout the county as a grisly object lesson. Some 284 were enslaved and transported to the West Indies amidst horrific conditions.[10]

James may have won the battle, but he lost the figurative war. Increasingly dictatorial, he greatly exacerbated already internecine religious tensions by installing Catholic supporters in key governmental positions.

By the summer of 1688, a group of Protestant noblemen appealed to Prince William of Orange (whose wife, Mary, was a safely Protestant heir to the British throne) to stage an invasion. William's forces landed on November 5, and the Glorious Revolution—or Bloodless Revolution, as it is sometimes called—ensued. The disgraced James sought sanctuary in France, where King Louis XIV gave him a home and generous pension. In many ways, it was the final chapter of the religious conflicts and wars that had followed Henry VIII's death many years before in 1547. Britain and her people were finally accorded a measure of peace.

John Bunyan died on the eve of William's invasion. Just sixty years old, he never saw the onset of a political peace that might have graced his final years. Violence and bloodshed, persecution and upheaval—this was the only world he knew. It was a world that would twice imprison him. It was a world described in his masterwork, *The Pilgrim's Progress*. Against such a setting, the amazing thing is that he ever wrote a book at all.

A PARISH IN THE HUNDRED

Bunyan draws quite naturally on common life and the culture of the countryside . . . he can echo the very tones of the parables, because he has grown up close to the soil.[1]

—Roger Sharrock

When traveling on the Bedford Southern Bypass, one might hardly notice the sign marking the tiny hamlet of Harrowden, England. It is, literally, a "one-street hamlet" that runs from east to west parallel and to the south of the A421.[2] Nestled in a low hillside, Harrowden is so unassuming a place that it seems almost entirely overshadowed by two giant hangars that dominate the horizon—imposing reminders of the days of Britain's airship industry. It was from Harrowden that the ill-fated R-101 airship departed on its maiden voyage in 1930, crashing in northern France with the tragic loss of forty-eight lives—the death toll surpassing even that of the *Hindenburg*'s fiery demise seven years later.[3]

Today, Harrowden—the name comes from the Anglo-Saxon word *Hearg-dūn*, meaning "Temple Hill"—is a place of thatched cottages with whitewashed walls and neatly kept gardens. Close by, checkerboard cornfields with alternating hues of green and amber bear witness to the region's agricultural past and present. It is in one of these cornfields that a stone marker can be found—a rough-hewn, red stone reminder of Harrowden's greatest claim to fame. For it was here, in the late summer or early autumn of 1628, that Bunyan was born. The legend on the stone reads simply: "This stone was erected in the Festival of Britain Year to mark the birthplace of John Bunyan, 1628–1688."

≈

Harrowden is where the cottage that was Bunyan's birthplace once stood. But the nearby village of Elstow (one mile southwest) is the place most closely associated with the years of his youth. There, in the abbey church of St. Mary and St. Helena, one may see the Norman-era font in which he was baptized. It was there that he and his family worshiped during his boyhood.

The abbey was found in 1078 by Countess Judith, a favored niece of William the Conqueror. In time, it became one of the richest of Benedictine nunneries. When the dissolution of the monasteries took place during Henry VIII's reign, St. Mary and St. Helena ceased to be an abbey. It was substantially reduced in size during the reign of Elizabeth I. Its dimensions today date from that time, and it is now a parish church graced with a lovely green. Still, during the 1630s, the years of Bunyan's youth, memories of what the former abbey had been were relatively fresh—as were memories of the religious strife that had so altered its fate and appearance.

"Elstow, a parish in the hundred of Redbornstoke, county of Bedford, one quarter mile from Bedford, containing 548 inhabitants." So reads Samuel Lewis's description of the village where Bunyan was born, as featured in *A Topographical Dictionary of England* (published in 1831).

When Samuel Lewis put pen to paper, Elstow was little changed from Bunyan's time. When the Reverend John Brown wrote his authoritative and copious biography fifty-four years later, *John Bunyan: His Life, Times and Work*, Elstow's defiance of change and the march of time had continued unabated.

It is worth taking time to talk about John Brown. Perhaps Bunyan's most assiduous biographer, he is still one of the most important. And though his substantial tome was published in 1885—the copy I have before me runs to 504 pages of close-set ten-point type—he has placed all scholars of Bunyan in his debt. A successor to Bunyan in pastoral ministry at Bedford, and keeper of such Bunyan relics and documents as had survived into the late nineteenth century, he was ideally placed (and suited) to write his biography. The impression one gets when leafing through his handsome, carefully documented work is that of a man who has undertaken his own pilgrimage—seeking to recover, as much as can be done, all of the sights, sounds, and settings that shaped John Bunyan.

Brown performed his task admirably. The table is set when

we encounter a title-page companion illustration taken from Robert White's superb line drawing of Bunyan. It is an arresting image. One's attention is drawn immediately to the eyes, which are at once purposeful and charismatic. White presents us with a Bunyan who looks very contemporary. In his sparing use of lines, he evokes a hint of the Puritan garb Bunyan wore. But our focus, as it should be, is drawn to Bunyan's face, the most fully realized aspect of the drawing. There are hidden depths here, and a glimpse of the racy wit that Bunyan surely possessed. Another quality is present as well—sturdiness is the word that comes to mind. Here is a man who can lean into the wind amidst a storm. He will not break.

But Brown was not merely adept in his choice of images or use of documentary sources. He had a pastor's gift for crafting word pictures—scenes that allow the reader to accompany him on his tour of Bunyanesque landscapes.

We see this, for example, in the second chapter of his book. "Elstow," we read,

> a little more than a mile to the south-west of Bedford, is a quaint, quietly nestling place . . . Fronting the road-side, with overhanging storeys and gabled dormers, are half-timbered cottages . . . The long building in the centre of the village . . . with projecting upper chambers and central overhanging gateway, still retains much of the external appearance it presented as a hostelry for pilgrims in pre-Reformation times. Opposite to the gate of this hostelry is the opening to the village green, on the north side of which stands what we may call the Moot Hall of the parish, a picturesque building of

timber and brick, which, with its oaken beams bearing traces of perpendicular carving and its ruddy tiles touched here and there with many-tinted lichen, presents to the eye in the summer sunlight a pleasant combination of colour and form.

This curious structure of fifteenth-century work, furnishing a somewhat fine example of the domestic architecture of the period, was probably originally erected to serve as the *hospitium* for travellers, and while not far from the road [it] was yet within the *ballium* or outer court of Elstow Abbey. At a later time . . . it was the scene also of village festivities, statute hirings, and all the public occasions of village life.[4]

Westward from the Moot Hall was a more substantial village green. At its center, still to be seen today, is the pedestal and broken stem of the ancient stone market cross round which were held fairs in May relished by the villagers of Elstow and beyond. Such had been the custom for hundreds of years, since the mid-twelfth century and the reign of King Henry II. At such times the fair would spill out from the green and absorb the nearby streets. Merchandise of all kinds would be displayed. Jugglers and puppet shows provided entertainment. Perhaps a play would be performed on a specially constructed stage. Children and adults would be regaled with carnival demonstrations: feats of strength, sleight of hand, and an entire repertoire of magician's tricks. The whole, grand spectacle was a highlight of the year.[5]

The same village green upon which the May fairs were held was extensive enough for John Bunyan and other children to take part in summer games and dancing. There were spirited contests of football (soccer), as well, that sometimes verged on violence.[6] Other games included trapball and Northern murr and spell.[7] And always, so far as John Bunyan was concerned, there were bouts of his favorite game, tipcat.[8]

And what of Elstow itself? How did it come by its name? Elstow, we learn, or Helenstow, was "the *stow* or stockaded place of St. Helen, a name cognate to such forms as Bridestow and Morwenstow." Helenstow "was so called because of the dedication of the old Saxon church to Helena, the mother of Constantine the Great."[9]

The fortunes of religious conflict left one visible and graphic reminder on Elstow Green: the stump of a cross damaged during the Reformation. Still visible today, it marks the site on the green where the annual May Fair used to be held. There, each year of his boyhood, Bunyan would have observed "the merchants, jugglers, actors and rogues who attended the fairs"—scenes that later found such vivid expression in *The Pilgrim's Progress*. It was also on this green that Bunyan, along with the other young people of the village, would have played for hours. A good athlete, he was particularly skilled in the game of tipcat—a form of rounders played with a stick instead of a ball.[10]

The classic 1911 edition of the *Encyclopedia Britannica* tells us that tipcat is a game where "the batter, having placed the billet, or 'cat' (a small chunk of wood), in a small circle on the ground, tips it into the air and hits it to a distance. His opponent then offers him a certain number of points, based upon his estimate of the number of hops or jumps necessary to cover the distance." The current edition of the EB reports that tipcat dates back at least to the seventeenth century and was introduced to North America by English colonists.[11]

Other elements of the local landscape shaped Bunyan's life and fixed themselves in his memory. Elstow Brook is a rivulet he would have known well. He and his family would have crossed it countless times as they walked the mile to Elstow village and the abbey church from their home.[12] Another body of water he would have known was the River Great Ouse in Bedford, meandering as it does through sleepy bywaters before broadening into deeper channels bordered by grassy banks and agèd trees.

So emerges a picture of the world Bunyan knew—a place of ancient importance, a center of religious history, a prosperous place with more than its share of the pastoral. It was a place possessed of scenes that left a lasting impression—scenes that lingered on in the mind of a boy whose imaginative gifts would one day make them familiar to readers in the millions.

A GOODLY HERITAGE

> [A] little roadside dwelling in the village of Elstow
> [is] still pointed out as Bunyan's cottage. Within
> living memory it was a thatched building with a
> lean-to forge at the south end.[1]
>
> —John Brown

Bunyan's family had ancient connections to Elstow.
Records show that in 1199 a worthy named William
Bonyun rented land from the Abbess there.[2] Curious
spellings of the Bunyan surname appear down through the
years, and Bunyan's father, Thomas, was not exempt from the
fanciful renderings. In 1603 the Vicar of Elstow registered his
birth under the name Thomas *Bonnionn*.[3]

Thomas and Margaret Bunyan, parents of John, were
married in the abbey church on May 23, 1627. It was a second
marriage for Thomas. His first wife, Anne, had died childless
earlier the same year.[4]

Thomas and Margaret's marriage seems to have been happy, and there were reasons enough to think it would remain so. Margaret, like Thomas, was a native of Elstow. Born Margaret Bentley in 1603, she had known Thomas Bunyan all her life. That the Bentleys and Bunyans were close families was reinforced when Margaret's sister, Rose, married Thomas's brother, Edward, in 1628. There was, then, an extended family of close-knit relations for Thomas and Margaret's children to know.

The union of Margaret and Thomas was soon blessed with three children in five years. John, their eldest child, was born in the late summer or early autumn of 1628. A sister, named after her mother, was born in 1630; a brother, William, was born in 1633. Three little faces to make any couple happy, much-loved reasons to cherish hopes for the future.

Still one wishes to know more about John Bunyan's parents. For a start, we know too little about his mother, Margaret. However, from the scant sources available, it is possible to discern some things.

The will of her mother, Mary Bentley (who died in 1632), reveals that Margaret "came not of the very squalid poor, but of people who, though humble in station, were yet decent and worthy in their ways, and took an honourable pride in the simple belongings of their village home."[5]

We have been given a glimpse of what Margaret Bunyan might have been like. John Brown wrote, "The mother of a child so much above the common kind must herself have been a woman of more than common power." Building on this supposition, Brown continued: "We should not be surprised to be told that she was one of those strongly-marked personalities sometimes met with in English village life—a woman of racy, ready wit, and of picturesque power of expression, who, [like] Mrs. Poyser [in Eliot's novel *Adam Bede*], had a very distinct individuality of her own, and the capacity of making a very distinct impression upon those around her." Brown's last observation is as haunting as it is succinct: "unfortunately to us she is little more than a name."

Reading this, one is reminded of that moving passage from E. M. Forster's domestic biography *Marianne Thornton* in which he wrote of his great-great-grandmother: "I possess a poignant fragment of her diary, in which she sees, with terrible clarity, that the time must come when it will not be known that Lucy Thornton ever lived. She stands on the brink of an oblivion which frightened her."[6]

We have no description, however fleeting, of Margaret's appearance. It is possible, though, to hazard a guess as to what faith she may have possessed. Robert Southey, Poet Laureate and an early nineteenth-century biographer of Bunyan, wrote that his parents took "some pains [to] impress . . . him with a sense of his religious duties" when he was a boy. Otherwise, Southey reasoned, when the young Bunyan later became "proficient in cursing and swearing," he would not have been visited by feelings of remorse.[7] It is a plausible conjecture.

The last thing we can deduce about Margaret Bunyan is that she was an affectionate mother. She died when John was sixteen, and he took the news particularly hard. This sense of loss was compounded when his father remarried within months. Thomas Bunyan can be forgiven for this. He had two younger children to raise; necessity compelled him.

But John, too young to appreciate his father's plight but old enough to deeply mourn an affectionate mother, resented his father's decision.[8] He could only feel that his father had remarried with indecent haste and committed an indignity upon his mother's memory.

The picture of Margaret Bunyan that emerges is one of a woman Thomas Bunyan and his children would have mourned deeply. Born to a family of "humble station," she was, like them, "decent and worthy in [her] ways." Judging by the man John Bunyan became, it is plausible to assume her personality was something like his. She would have been "a woman of racy, ready wit, and picturesque power of expression"—a woman who "had a very distinct individuality . . . and the capacity of making a distinct impression upon those around her."[9] She made sure her eldest son could read and write. Her interest in religion, however modest, was such that she instilled some sense of basic religious duties in her son.[10] These things took place in an atmosphere of affection that made her son cherish her memory. But when all this is said—and it is not negligible—one still wishes to learn more about a woman who gave the world such a remarkable son.

5

THE TINKER OF ELSTOW

Thomas Bunyan . . . working at his forge by the
cottage in the fields, repairing the tools and utensils
of his neighbours at Elstow or Harrowden, or
wandering for the purposes of his trade from one
lonely farmhouse to another . . . would be neither
better nor worse than the rest of the craftsmen of the
hammer and the forge.[1]

—John Brown

homas Bunyan, John's father, is little less of a mystery
to us today than his mother. Though often described as
a tinker, he described himself in his will as a "braseyer,"
or brazier.[2] The original edition of *The Dictionary of National
Biography* states that Thomas Bunyan "was what we should now
call a whitesmith, a maker and mender of pots and kettles."[3]

The word *braseyer* has its origins in the old English
word *bræsi(an)*, which means "to work in brass." The most

straightforward meaning of the word is one who makes or repairs brass utensils of various kinds. Some braziers worked in pewter as well.[4]

Thomas Bunyan worked primarily in brass as he labored at his cottage-side forge and workshop. Sometimes working in tin and pewter, he would have most often made or repaired pots, pans, kettles, tools, and other kinds of common household utensils. A tradesman by profession, he was also a small freeholder—owning the cottage where his family lived, as well as the forge and workshop where he plied his trade.[5]

Lord Macaulay, in his classic biographical essay, tells us that tinkers were a hereditary caste, and there is no reason to think that braziers were not as well. This explains why John Bunyan, once he had learned to read and write, would have been taught the trade his father followed. It was expected.

What was the brazier's trade like? Here again we turn to John Brown, whose painstaking research has yielded a revealing portrait. Thomas Bunyan, Brown wrote, could be found most days "working at his forge by the cottage in the fields, repairing the tools and utensils of his neighbours at Elstow or Harrowden, or wandering for the purposes of his trade from one [scattered] farmhouse to another."[6]

Brown next draws our attention to *The Tinker of Turvey*, "a well-known character of those times," and suggests that this literary Tinker may not have been so very different from Thomas Bunyan. *The Tinker of Turvey*, we learn,

> lived some half-dozen miles away [from Elstow], across the fields, and is supposed, in the year of grace 1630, to have

"hammered out an epistle to all strolling Tinckers and all brave mettle-men that travel on the Hoofe." He boasts of the country he has bestridden, the towns he has traversed, and of the fairs in which he has been drunk. He claims that "all music first came from the hammer," that "the tincker is a rare fellow," for that "he is a scholler and was of Brazen-nose Colledge in Oxford, an excellent carpenter, for he builded Coppersmith's Hall."[7]

Thomas Bunyan, Brown continued:

may not have been . . . the roystering blade this brother "mettle-man" was, but in the course of his rounds he would meet with him and the like of him, and under the trees of the village green or on the settle of the village inn could probably tell as good a story and perhaps drink as deep.[8]

If all of this conjures a picture of Thomas Bunyan looking rather like a village blacksmith, the image is not far amiss. His days started early, perhaps before sunrise. The fire in his forge needed to be stoked or started anew, and kept alight throughout the course of a long, tiring day. There would have been a grimy aspect to his work, more than a little muck, muscle, and sweat as the bellows were worked and the hammer swung. Patience, perseverance, and a willingness to begin again should the tool being forged not look quite right—these things were needed, as well as strength and stamina. It was not easy to follow the brazier's trade.

Seemingly at odds with these images is the realization that

a brazier was also an artisan. True enough, pots, pans, kettles, tools, and other kinds of household utensils had a rather pedestrian purpose. But that did not mean that they were nondescript in appearance. Thomas Bunyan would have taken pride in his work and shown much skill in it. Had he not, he would not have been in business for long or have maintained the tradition of excellence or pride in one's work that was supposed to attend a trade passed from father to son.

Aside from this, a somewhat apocryphal story has come down to us about Thomas Bunyan. It is worth recounting, if only for the hereditary traits it might attest.

In the parish next to Elstow, Houghton Conquest, lived a rector by the name of Thomas Archer—a king's chaplain with a keen interest in nature. As such, we learn that he kept "a sort of *chronicon mirabile* [or parish record] of the little rural world in which his tranquil days were spent."[9]

Sometime in the spring of 1625, word reached Archer of a rare natural phenomenon. It so captured his fancy that he recorded what he had heard. "One Bonion of Elsto," he scratched across the parchment with the nib of his quill pen, "clyminge of Rookes neasts in the Bery wood found 3 Rookes in a nest, all white as milke and not a blacke fether on them."[10]

It is a brief entry, but it affords a priceless glimpse into a life that is in so many ways silent. Perhaps on his way home from a farmhouse call, Thomas Bunyan dismounted to let his horse graze in a meadow near Ellensbury Wood. Hearing a bit of birdsong, he looked up and saw the three milk-white birds in a black rook's nest. Struck by the rarity of the sight, he climbed the tree where the nest was. Carefully, he peered in at the nestlings, thinking that he had never seen the like, and perhaps never would see such a sight again.[11]

He returned home full of the story, regaling his wife and neighbors with the tale in the days that followed. Word eventually reached Houghton Conquest and Thomas Archer.

What is revealing about this is the sensitivity and thoughtfulness it betokens. Knowing what we know about John Bunyan's artistry, however rustic its origins, it is difficult to not think that he inherited a sensitivity and thoughtfulness from his father: an artisan's temperament and gifts. One thinks as well of how seldom we meet with such homely vignettes in documentary sources that have come down to us from the early 1600s. For all of these reasons, it is a lovely story.

One last picture meets our eyes as we think of a day shortly following the birth of the brazier's son—that of a chilly day in November 1628. On the morning of the thirtieth, Thomas and Margaret dressed baby John warmly and walked with him to the Elstow church.[12] Exchanging happy looks, they crossed the village green and walked past trees in their late autumn tints. Thomas lived in a cottage and toiled at a forge. But it was an honest trade and one of which he was proud. Now, after the harrowing loss of his first wife, and a happy second marriage, he could carry his firstborn to church. He would do what he could to set his son firmly on the road that lay ahead.

"THE GLAD REASON
OF LIFE"[1]

This fond attachment to the well-known place
Whence first we started into life's long race,
Maintains its hold with such unfailing sway,
We feel it even in age, and at our latest day.[2]

—William Cowper

In myriad ways, the landscape and culture of the English Midlands gave rise to the imaginative world of *The Pilgrim's Progress*. "The tract of country between the Trent and the Bedfordshire Ouse," biographer John Brown wrote, was a land of fields and fens.[3] Its northern half bequeathed two Pilgrim Fathers to New England—one of whom was Peter Bulkeley, the great-grandfather of Ralph Waldo Emerson—whilst its southern reaches were peopled by men known for their sturdy independence of thought, and strong sympathy for the Puritan faith.[4]

In Bunyan's youth, Bedfordshire was also staunchly Protestant. This was true of tradespeople in the towns, and a majority of the gentry in the country-houses. The Earls of Kent and Bedford were steadfastly Protestant in their religious commitments.[5]

More than this, Bedfordshire was "a recognised asylum of religious liberty. Refugees for conscience' sake," Brown wrote:

> came from Alençon and Valenciennes, and settled at Cranfield in 1568, bringing with them their lace pillows, and establishing the lace trade of the district . . . Many Protestants from the Netherlands, fleeing from Philip of Spain and the Duke of Alva . . . found a home in the villages of Bedfordshire, introducing names still to be recognised in the parish registers, collections were also made in the churches of the county for others still in their own land, and still suffering cruel hardships on account of their faith.[6]

There was, then, in Bunyan's time, a pervasive sensibility regarding matters of religious conscience. Bedfordshire was an internationally recognized haven for people fleeing persecution. Bunyan likely would have encountered families whose lives had been touched by religious persecution.

What of the other denizens of Bedfordshire? We learn from the "Act-Books" of the Archdeacons' Courts that not everyone was particularly pious or noble. These record books, kept for hundreds of years down to the year 1640, attest a close scrutiny "of the lives of the people in each parish of each of the deaneries of which the archdeaconry was composed. These Courts, which were regularly held, took note of every conceivable offence against morals as well as against ecclesiastical discipline."[7]

Many cases in the Act-Books dealt with "matters of intemperance and impurity"—euphemisms for drunkenness and sexual sins such as fornication and adultery. Other transgressions fell into the category of local color. One hapless man ran afoul of the local authorities for "folding some sheep in the church during a snow storm"—that is to say he sheltered his sheep in church to keep them safe from the ravages of a winter storm. One feels for him. His life, and that of his family, was dependent on his sheep.

Still other censures and punishments as were meted out reveal something of pastimes and occupations Bunyan would have known well. Sometime between 1610 and 1617—within twenty years of his birth—two men, Oliver Lenton and Walter Lewin of Barford, were punished for "looking on football players on Sunday." John Hawkes of Renhold was punished for "playing at nineholes" on the Sabbath.[8]

Saints' days were no less rigorously observed. "Three parishioners of Milton Ernys," John Brown wrote, "came under the lash of the court: Leonard Willimot for carting on St. Luke's day; James Haiey, for winnowing corn on Easter Tuesday; and Walter Griffin for putting upp netts and catching larks on a holiday." John Neele of Luton found to his dismay that he had done wrong in "stocking a fruit tree on All Saints' day," as did also Thomas Bigrave of Pavenham, and John West of Stevington, who were "at a foote-ball plaie on Ascension Day." All three were summarily fined.[9]

Such accounts reveal that in many ways the experiences of John Bunyan's boyhood were those to be found in typical county village.[10] Saints and sinners, cheek by jowl—many pious, many not—not a few somewhere in between.

An eldest child, Bunyan had a sister, Margaret, and a brother, William. Three active children, then, were companions and rivals under the same thatched roof.[11] Hours of play and learning to do chores under their parents' watchful eye—butter churning and learning to keep the forge fire burning among them.

The Bunyan cottage, we learn, "stood in a field at the foot of a gentle slope, from which the tower of Elstow Church a mile away was plainly visible." Other distinctives of the local landscape were close at hand. "In nearer distance," we learn from Bunyan's Pulitzer Prize–winning biographer Ola Winslow,

> were other thatched cottages similar to that of Thomas Bunyan. By walking to the end of the slope he could see the spire of St. Paul's Church in Bedford, scarcely further than a mile away also. Except for marginal glimpses such as these, however, and the human associations they represented, life was little wider than the immediate cottage neighborhood. Bunyan's End [where the family resided] was a dead-end street, and the village of Elstow, number[ed] no more than sixty families.[12]

Celia Fiennes, a "sidesaddle traveler" of gentle birth who rode through Bedfordshire within ten years of Bunyan's death in 1688, has left a written account that opens a window on the world of Bedford, the town in close proximity to Elstow that played such a significant part in Bunyan's life.

The daughter of a colonel in Cromwell's army, Celia Fiennes was said to have ridden through every county in England, accompanied only by two servants. In 1697 and 1698 she made two long journeys through northern England and Scotland. Traveling to improve her health, she visited many spa towns. But she was also bent on personal adventure. Hers was a remarkable series of journeys, and she a remarkable literary pioneer.[13]

Her descriptions of Bedford and its environs evoke a now-distant past. She saw streets that were "small and old," houses on Bedford Bridge, and took note of the "very good fish" that swam in the Ouse—"taken out fresh for supper or dinner." On the banks of the river were "notches of ground" set with willows, with little boats chained under their branches.[14]

Moving to the town center, she observed the "well kept bowling green" and nearby summer houses. Climbing to the top of the market house, she was afforded a prospect that commanded the "whole town and Country round." It was a pleasant prospect, and a pleasant cluster as well of village life and all its shared experiences. It was a prospect John Bunyan knew and loved as a boy—one that lived on in his memory.

"Clearly," Ola Winslow wrote of Bunyan, "the imagination of this gifted boy had been nourished by country fact." Then follows a description of what those country facts were, the "sound of bells across the valley," and with them

> wide spaces, secret dells, rocky slopes, fields stretching far away. There is dew on the grass, the music of brooks, a child's fear of dark places, the footprint of animals at dawn, a

bundle of myrrh for the gathering, a robin with a spider in its mouth. The evidence of such association as belongs to one's early years.[15]

Bunyan would one day become an artist whose best writing was marked by a vivid literary imagination—evoking scenes and images through word pictures that fastened themselves upon the memory. Clearly, there was much about the environment of his youth to nurture and stimulate his gifts.

SCHOLARSHIP OF THE SLENDEREST KIND

I am always for getting a boy forward in his learning, for that is sure good. I would let him at first read any English book which happens to engage his attention; because you have done a great deal when you have brought him to have entertainment from a book. He'll get better books afterwards.[1]

—Samuel Johnson

In the citation above, Samuel Johnson might well have been describing John Bunyan. For while his was only a rudimentary education, the influence of books that then captured his imagination stayed with him far longer than many of his schoolboy lessons.

Bunyan wrote almost nothing about his days at school, commencing his autobiography, *Grace Abounding*, with only "a hint of my pedigree and manner of bringing up."[2]

The story was not long in the telling. "My father's house," he wrote, was "of that rank that is meanest and most despised . . . yet . . . it pleased God to [prompt my parents] to put me to school, to learn me both to read and write . . . according to the rate of other poor men's children."[3]

It is a modest and slender account. But what little is there is revealing. First, there is a note of gratitude—a sense that his parents, despite their humble station, had done what they could to give him a good start in life. There seems to be an awareness, too, that braseyers' sons seldom went to school, and that Providence had smiled upon him in a way that was rare.

But there seems to be something more as well: a tinge of unmistakable regret. Yes, he had learned to read and write. But it was, nonetheless, "according to the rate of other poor men's children."[4] Other men's children—wealthier men's children—continued on in their schooling. He did not. But he had glimpsed, however briefly, a wider world. He was a child of keen intelligence and an artist's gifts. He would have relished the vistas of that wider world in a way that few children did. Yet, when his formal schooling stopped, that door closed. It must have been a bitter blow.

This tinge of regret recalls the words of yet another supremely gifted writer of humble origins. In 1860, when Abraham Lincoln was asked if he would allow a campaign biography to be written, he replied: "it is a great piece of folly to attempt to make anything out of my early life. It can all be condensed into a single sentence [from] Gray's *Elegy*: 'the short and simple annals of the poor.' That's my life, and that's all you or anyone else can make of it."[5]

But as with Lincoln, whose hardscrabble education was painstakingly gained, Bunyan refused to let the door that had closed upon his formal education stay shut. Through the few books that he was able to read after his time at school, the door remained open for a time, if only a little. These books fed his imagination and left impressions that lingered on because the experiences they afforded were so rare.

Here Lord Macaulay provides an insight that helps us to understand this side of Bunyan's early life. He wrote that Bunyan's father "was more respectable than most [tinkers]," that he had "a fixed residence, and was able to send his son to . . . school."[6]

Macaulay was right to draw attention to this. Tinkers, if they were known for anything at all, were generally regarded as traveling tradesman—going from town to town hawking their wares or offering their services. They were often viewed in a less generous light—prevailing wisdom held them to be "vagrants and pilferers [who] were often confounded with gypsies"[7]— with Sir Walter Scott being perhaps the most famous writer to have perpetuated this popular misconception.[8]

Thomas Bunyan, as the head of a family with ancient ties to Elstow, and the owner of a yeoman's cottage[9] and forge, would have stood out among his fellow braseyers. True enough, he traveled about from time to time to offer his services.[10] But he had a base of operations, and reason to think that being settled as he was, he could build upon this foundation and steadily advance his family's fortunes. He was a village braseyer, a local businessman, not solely an itinerant tradesman.

Beyond this, he had determined that his eldest son would go to school. Not for long, perhaps only a year or a little better than that, but time enough to learn to read and write. It would be more than he had, and that was something—a place to start.[11]

John Bunyan's schooldays may have been fleeting, but we know that he developed a lifelong love of reading that first manifested itself in a fondness for a kind of cheap pamphlet known as a chapbook.[12] And given the ways in which chapbooks shaped his moral and creative imagination, it is worth taking some time to talk about them.

Chapbooks were an early form of popular literature. The words *chapbook* and *chapman* are derived from the Anglo-Saxon word *céap*, the word for buying and selling. In the nineteenth century, the word *chapbook* was formally recognized by bibliophiles as a word referring to many kinds of printed material—pamphlets, political and religious tracts, nursery rhymes, poetry, folk tales, and almanacs. More often than not, such writings were illustrated with woodcuts and other such rough-hewn images.

In Bunyan's time, chapmen were peddlers—and chapbooks part of the stock they carried about in wagons from town to town. Because his father was a respected local businessman, peddlers were in and around the Bunyan cottage frequently. Visits of chapmen to the Bunyan home would have been commonplace; every month or so one would stop by—perhaps more often than that.

Happy as the thought is of these little books making their way about the kingdom, their very commonplace nature explains why so few survive today. Most who acquired chapbooks had no thought of amassing formal libraries—certainly not with books of such flimsy and indifferent quality. Consequently, they were put to other uses—some rather pedestrian, others more ignoble. Some chapbooks became wrappers for baked goods—rather like getting one's fish and chips in a newspaper—others became what contemporary sources called *bum fodder* (i.e., toilet paper).[13]

For the most part, they were small paper-covered booklets, printed on a single sheet folded into books of eight, twelve, sixteen, and twenty-four pages. Often, they were illustrated with crude woodcuts.[14] Chapbooks varied widely in quality—both in terms of content and presentation. A noted collector of chapbooks, Harry Weiss, once observed: "the printing in many cases was execrable, the paper even worse, and the woodcut illustrations, some of which did duty for various tales regardless of their fitness, were sometimes worse than the paper and presswork combined."[15]

This was true enough, but some chapbooks ran to considerable length, were well produced, and in some cases were historically accurate. That Bunyan may have acquired one of these better-produced books seems plausible. For in his later writings he references Aristotle and Plato.

Bunyan may not have received formal schooling in the classics, but it is possible he encountered Aristotle and Plato in one of the better-produced chapbooks—in this case a popular work of history.

We know something about these works. The diarist Samuel Pepys,[16] for example, had his collection of chapbooks bound into volumes according to subject matter. One volume contained writings on *"History—true and fabulous."* We know, as well, that chapbook presentations of the mythic past were popular. Such books, whether about morality, history, or myth, would have had enough passages about Aristotle and Plato to whet a precocious boy's appetite and to prompt a wistful reference to them in later life, wishing he had learned more about them.

Crucially, chapbooks were priced for sale to workers, though their market was not limited to the working class. Broadside ballads were sold for a halfpenny, or a few pence.[17] Prices of chapbooks were from 2d. to 6d.—this at a time when agricultural labourers' wages were 12d. per day. It must be remembered, too, that literacy was not uncommon in early modern England. Many people of humble station were readers.

Chapbooks contributed significantly to the development of literacy. Francis Kirkman, Bunyan's contemporary, said they fired his imagination and his love of books.[18] There is further evidence of their use by other autodidacts in Kirkman and Bunyan's lifetimes—though they are two of the most noteworthy.

Chapbooks were printed in astonishing numbers. In the 1660s, as many as 400,000 almanacs were printed annually, enough for one family in three in England.[19] A conservative estimate of their sales in Scotland alone in the second half of the eighteenth century was over 200,000 per year.

Printers provided chapbooks to chapmen on credit.[20] Chapmen, in turn, carried them around the country, selling from door to door, at markets and fairs, and returning to pay for the stock they sold. This facilitated wide distribution and large sales with minimum outlay.[21] It also told the printers which titles were bestsellers. Popular works were reprinted, pirated, edited, and produced in different editions.

In 1597, certain chapbooks began being marketed specifically for an audience of clothiers, weavers, and shoemakers, which is significant when we remember Bunyan's background as the son of a braseyer. The rationale was simple: clothiers, weavers, and shoemakers were becoming increasingly literate. In 1612 Thomas Deloney,[22] a weaver, wrote *Thomas of Reading*, a story about a band of six clothiers and what befell them when they met up with another group of clothiers at Basingstoke. Another of Deloney's stories, *Jack of Newbury*, was set in Henry VIII's time. It tells the tale of Jack, a broadcloth weaver's apprentice who takes over his master's business and marries his widow upon his death. Achieving success, Jack is known henceforth for his generosity to the poor. King Henry takes note of this and offers him a knighthood. Jack, in token of his true nobility, gallantly refuses. It is the kind of story a braseyer's son would have read and enjoyed.[23]

So why this digression, colorful though it may be, into a discussion of chapbooks? Simply this: what John Bunyan read in chapbooks formed the first of two major literary streams that flowed into the masterwork that became *The Pilgrim's Progress*. Take away the influence of chapbooks upon Bunyan's literary imagination and *The Pilgrim's Progress* would never have been written.[24]

Since the Bunyans had slender financial resources, they may have bartered for the wares a chapman carried about with him. One can see how a young boy with intellectual curiosity and a vivid imagination, as we know John was, might have asked his father often if he could purchase a chapbook. It was as though a traveling library had come through the village and opened a window to another world—a world he had left all too soon and wished to revisit. John's formal schooling may have ceased, but his hunger to learn—and to imagine—did not.

What were the chapbooks Bunyan read? We know of two, referenced in one of his early works.[25] "Give me a ballad, a newsbook," a character in this book stated, "*George on horseback* or *Bevis of Southampton*; give me some book that teaches curious arts, that tells of old fables."[26]

And so Bunyan was familiar with two of the best-known legends of chivalric romance: the cycle of tales surrounding St. George and the dragon and the far-flung exploits of the knight known as Bevis of Southampton.

The tales of St. George have an iconic place in the European imagination. He is the patron saint of England, and many other countries. There are many legends surrounding his exploits.

The central myth arose from tales told by crusader knights. According to this story, a dragon made its nest near the spring that provided water for the city of Silene. This beast was a bloodthirsty creature, and the only way the people of Silene could draw their daily water was to lure the dragon away from the spring, which they did by offering a human sacrifice. Hapless victims were chosen by the drawing of lots. No one was exempt.

One day, the name of the royal princess was drawn. Her father, the king, begged for her life—but to no avail. She was taken to the dragon. But just when all seemed lost, St. George arrived (his soldierly travels having taken him to Silene). He confronted the dragon and killed it, following an epic struggle. Upon restoring the princess to her father, the entire city was caught up in this miraculous deliverance. They renounced their pagan beliefs and converted to Christianity.[27]

The legends surrounding Bevis of Southampton are less well known today, but they were widely known in the world of seventeenth-century Europe. These tales (which assumed their most popular form sometime in the fourteenth century) are said to comprise a chivalric romance "that has it all."[28] The central motifs include:

a hero whose exploits take him from callow youth to hard-won maturity . . . a resourceful and appealing heroine; faithful servants and dynastic intrigue; a parade of interesting villains, foreign and domestic, exotic and local; a geographical sweep which moves back and forth from England to the Near East and through most of western Europe; battles with dragons and giants; forced marriages . . . disguises and mistaken identities; harsh imprisonments with dramatic escapes, harrowing rescues . . . and, last but not least, a horse of such valor that his death at the end of the [story] is at least as tragic as that of the heroine, and almost as tragic as that of [the hero] himself.[29]

The slaying of dragons . . . the quests of knights-errant . . . rescues from unjust imprisonment . . . the perseverance, despite many trials, of true love—tragic deaths, faith that could triumph over bitter adversity and suffering—such was the world that captured the boyish imagination of John Bunyan. We know as well that he read stories (though we don't know their names) of "curious arts, [and] old fables."[30] It was a world of magic, adventure, faith, and martial courage—all intermingled. It was a world that drew him away, perhaps, to a favorite spot by the water or meadow, where these tales could prompt his imagination to take flight. What is more, unlike many men of his class, Thomas Bunyan was in a position to grant his son's wishes to acquire a little library. Chapbooks began to come into the Bunyan household. Through them, John Bunyan's love of reading could find an outlet. His life of the mind could continue yet a while longer.

DISQUIETING INTIMATIONS

It is not wonderful, therefore, that [John Bunyan,] a
lad to whom nature had given a powerful imagination
and sensibility which amounted to a disease, should
have been early haunted by religious terrors.[1]

—Thomas Babington (Lord Macaulay)

Bunyan's youth seems somewhat idyllic. And in certain
respects it was—else so many of the good things he had
known and experienced during those years would not
have lived on in the pages of *The Pilgrim's Progress*—faithfully
rendered scenes of country life and the winsome folkways of the
midlands among them.

But there was another and darker side to Bunyan's childhood. For a time during his preadolescent years, he was subject
to what he called "fearful dreams."[2] These were "dreadful

visions . . . apprehensions of Devils, and wicked spirits, who . . . laboured to draw me away with them."[3] Day and night, he was "greatly troubled and afflicted" by fears of the day of judgment and thoughts of an eternity amidst the torments of "fire, Devils and Hellish Fiends."[4]

What triggered such dreams? This much we know: Bunyan was a highly intelligent and impressionable child, with sensitivities that would later reveal themselves to be artistic in nature. He had a vivid, perhaps photographic memory, as his later recasting of chapbook legends in *The Pilgrim's Progress* attests. He may also have heard an apocalyptic message (or series of messages) from an overzealous preacher, or read a particularly lurid religious broadside or printed sermon.[5] If so, horrific images conjured in his imagination could have imprinted themselves in deeply troubling and persistent ways. A boy deferential to authority and trusting of his elders could easily place too much credence in dire statements by an authority figure or the apocalyptic pronouncements of a broadside. A boy like Bunyan might well have believed that the things said in books or broadsides were always true and real.

Experiences like these could have conspired together, producing stress and a harrowing sense of fear that resurfaced in dreams. Contemporary research has shown that "sufferers of frequent nightmares tend to be creative people with an ability to depict their dreams in unusually real terms."[6] Many years before, in 1830, Robert Southey showed an intuitive grasp of Bunyan's malady when he quoted a phrase from *Grace Abounding*: "I was often much cast down," Bunyan had said, "and afflicted in my mind."[7] Lord Macaulay came closer still, saying: "It is not wonderful . . . that a lad to whom nature had given a powerful imagination and sensibility which amounted to a disease, should have been early haunted by religious terrors."[8]

Macaulay was more right than he knew. Bunyan's sensibility did in fact amount to a disease. For while terms such as "clinical depression" were not used in his time (Macaulay died in 1859), the condition known as melancholy was one that was generally known and recognized. What is more, in Bunyan's time as well as Macaulay's, melancholy was often associated with a pervasive sense of religious anxiety.

Thus melancholy, with a frequent, though not exclusively religious orientation, appears to have been the condition to which Bunyan was periodically subject throughout his life. Its first manifestation was in his preadolescent years; but then, his youthful resiliency also helped to quell its initial onset. This we learn from Bunyan himself: "A while after, these terrible dreams did leave me, which also I soon forgot, for my pleasures did quickly cut off the remembrance of them, as if they had never been."[9] In this way, Bunyan's childhood was not without a measure of grace—and there is a grace in such a forgetting.

In June 1644 he suffered the first great sorrow of his life when his mother died after a sudden onset of illness. Within a month his sister Margaret died, perhaps in her early teens, and there was another sad procession to a graveside.

These were crushing losses. Bunyan was in his formative years, and the bonds of affection ran deep within him.[10] A sensitive young man, his grief was keenly felt. There is a sad silence as to his feelings about the loss of his sister, Margaret. We know they played as children, attended fairs in May, and walked together amidst green fields and the village streets of Elstow. There would have been the sharing of childish hopes and fancies—and the sound of their laughter within the walls of the family cottage.

All this had been taken away with a horrible suddenness, and there is no pain quite like the sudden, awful awareness of mortality. The world is never the same—especially for a young man who sees the world with an artist's eye:

> The leaves of the oak and the willows shall fade,
> Be scattered around, and together be laid;
> And the young and the old, and the low and the high,
> Shall moulder to dust, and together shall lie.

> The child that a mother attended and loved,
> The mother that infant's affection that proved,
> The husband that mother and infant that blest,
> Each—all are away to their dwelling of rest.

> The maid on whose cheek, on whose brow, in whose eye,
> Shone beauty and pleasure—her triumphs are by:
> And the memory of those that beloved her and praised,
> Are alike from the minds of the living erased.[11]

Only one month after his wife's death, Thomas Bunyan remarried.[12] Even though young John may have understood that his father needed a wife to help raise his children and manage the household, this would have been a blow to him. His grief was still keen, and the wound it created still open and raw.

How Bunyan weathered all of this we do not know. He never wrote of the loss of his mother and sister, and it may be that he sustained a wound that always remained too tender to touch. We do know, however, that another great change would come within a matter of months. Even as he had suffered his first great sorrow, war was tearing England apart. The conflict would not be long in altering his life forever.

RUMORS OF WAR

From hence, let fierce contending nations know,
What dire effects from civil discord flow.[1]

—Joseph Addison

Bunyan's teenage years were overshadowed by civil war. On August 22, 1642, right around John's fourteenth birthday, Charles I raised the royal standard at Nottingham and gathered several thousand loyalist soldiers to his banner. In opposition, forces loyal to Parliament, some ten thousand soldiers in all, rallied to the standard raised by Robert Devereux, 3rd Earl of Essex. On September 23, portions of the two armies met in the first decisive cavalry engagement of the war—the battle of Powick Bridge. There a force of royalist cavalry under the command of Prince Rupert, about one thousand in all, defeated a Parliamentary cavalry detachment. So commenced a war that would last four long and tumultuous years, until Charles I's surrender to the Scottish army at Southwell, near Newark, on May 5, 1646.

For Bunyan, the ravages of this first English civil war remained the stuff of distant, disturbing news until he was sixteen—when the war came to his doorstep. Persuasive historical evidence suggests that he was drafted into the parliamentary army on or about November 30, 1644—just a few months after the deaths of his mother and sister.[2] He would remain in the army for the next three years.

Biographer John Brown related the set of circumstances that led to Bunyan's military service.

> It is . . . probable that as soon as [Bunyan] had reached the regulation age of sixteen he was included in one of the levies made by Parliament upon the villages of Bedfordshire, and without any choice of his own in the matter, was sent with others of his neighbours to the important garrison of Newport . . . The same ordinance of Parliament, which constituted Newport garrison, provided also that the county of Bedford, within fourteen days, shall send into it 225 able and armed men for souldiers.[3]

And so Bunyan's name was added to the muster rolls for the garrison of parliamentary forces at Newport Pagnell, Buckinghamshire. He began his service under the command of Colonel Richard Cockayne and remained there until March 8, 1645. He then appears to have been transferred to the command of Major Robert Bolton, where he remained until September 1646.[4] Bunyan concluded his military service under the command of Captain Charles O'Hara on July 21, 1647.[5]

According to the muster rolls, Bunyan was one of 128 "centinels" (or privates) in Cockayne's company.[6] Bunyan and his fellow centinels were to have a rude awakening. The conditions faced by Cockayne's troops, under the overall command of Sir Samuel Luke, were grim.[7] Just a few weeks before Bunyan's arrival, Luke had written to his superiors saying that without the provision of much-needed funds, his soldiers faced starvation. His letter closed ominously, with a blunt statement of his concerns about a possible mutiny.[8]

Surviving records indicate that between October 12, 1644, and November 26 of the same year, the numbers under Luke's command were increased by the arrival of some two hundred foot soldiers, of whom Bunyan was almost certainly one. If so, he would have become instantly aware of the hardships foot soldiers under Luke's command endured.[9] Low morale and insubordination were a constant source of concern. In January 1645 Colonel Cockayne reported to his superiors that his troopers were losing respect for him and his fellow officers. It is easy to see why. The soldiers were owed three and a half months of back pay. Many were forced to pawn their clothes and other personal possessions to buy bread.

Housing accommodations were scarcely better. Townsfolk in Bedfordshire had begun to refuse to house soldiers, because the soldiers themselves had no money to pay the homeowners with whom they hoped to find lodging. Conditions for the few who could find lodging were far from ideal. It was not unusual for soldiers to have to sleep "3 and 3 in a bed."[10] Beyond this, there was a serious shortage of boots, saddles, and horseshoes for the cavalry, which severely hampered their ability to take the field in force. Certain types of weapons were also in short supply, including muskets and pikes. Sir Samuel Luke communicated all of this to the commanding officer for Colonel Cockayne and his troops. The army in which Bunyan served was in dire straits.

It was at this time, in early February 1645, that Luke's worst fears were realized. A number of troops and dragoons mutinied. This partial uprising was quelled quickly, but that was a cold comfort. The scarcity of food for Luke's men was such that they could scarcely be supplied with the horsemeat and corn they had been reduced to eating. "The lamentations of the soldiers here," he wrote, "are so great through misery and want, that my pen is not able to express it."[11]

Meanwhile, Bunyan was receiving his basic training. He learned to march in formation,[12] form ranks in battle array, and use a musket. He was also probably armed with a handgun and trained in the use of a sword. When he had mastered these essential skills, he may have joined patrols sent out periodically in search of the enemy—though this seems somewhat unlikely, as such patrols were mostly comprised of cavalry. Still, it is worth noting that the kind of minor skirmishes that often took place during such missions had a high mortality rate, accounting for some 47 percent of the estimated deaths that took place during the English civil wars.[13]

Troops from the Newport garrison, of whom Bunyan was one, took part in two major engagements in May and early June 1645: the parliamentary siege of Oxford and an attack by royalist troops upon the city of Leicester. Tradition holds that Bunyan was nearly killed at Leicester, but this is incorrect.

Recent research indicates this experience almost certainly took place during the siege at Oxford.[14] Bunyan described this siege action and his narrow brush with death:

> When I was a Souldier, I with others were drawn out to go to such a place to besiege it; but when I was just ready to go, one of the company desired to go in my [place], to which, when I had consented he took my place, and coming to the siege, as he stood Sentinel, he was shot in the head with a Musket bullet and died.[15]

It was a mysterious providence—one Bunyan never forgot. His life had been spared in a remarkable way—though he did not yet know why. The awareness of this stayed with him far beyond the end of his military service in July 1647.

A NAMELESS LOVE

To no men are such cordial greetings given As those whose wives have made them fit for heaven.[1]

—Lord Byron

Within two years of his discharge from the parliamentary army, John Bunyan married. We do not know precisely when, since no record of the ceremony exists; but surviving documents tell us that Bunyan's first child, Mary, was christened on July 20, 1650. Since there is no reason to think the union was not immediately fruitful, it is plausible that Bunyan was married no later than October 1649.[2] It is a pleasing thought to envision the former soldier and his bride walking amidst fields and trees in the autumn on the way to their wedding. Perhaps there were flowers in her hair, and he wore clothes of the best homespun cloth.

But where did their wedding take place? The Elstow parish register contains no reference to such a ceremony. It is possible that the service was private and informal,[3] or that, according to the custom of the Commonwealth, they were married before some justice of the peace whose registers are lost.[4] The more likely explanation is that the wedding was held outside of Elstow parish because Bunyan's bride had been born and raised somewhere else.[5]

But if so, where was she raised? And what was her name? There are no records to tell us either answer, and it is a sober truth to acknowledge we can say nothing more. History has consigned this good lady to a sad oblivion.

Bunyan was himself partly to blame, since he never mentioned his wife's name in any published works or surviving manuscripts. This is surely not because he didn't love her. Rather, it may be that he loved her too well. She died while still a young woman, and the most likely explanation for Bunyan's silence is that her death was too painful to speak of. Some wounds run too deep to ever fully heal.

It is cheering to recall that several years passed before Bunyan and his wife were parted. Based on such writings as have survived, there is every reason to think these were largely happy years. John Brown has written of this as well as any biographer of Bunyan has:

> We know not who [Bunyan's wife] was, we do not even know her Christian name, but we do know that her advent brought [him] what he had not had since his mother's death, a real home brightened by the presence of love. It was not brightened by

much else. "This woman and I," says he, "came together as poor as poor might be, not having so much household stuff as a dish or spoon betwixt us both."

It was an unpromising beginning, but many that are more promising turn out worse. It may be that where there are health and hope and honest industry, mutual love and trust can better supply the lack of dish and spoon.[6]

However, these were soon supplied, perhaps fashioned by Bunyan himself. The making of pots, pans, and household utensils was his stock in trade.

Beyond this, there is every reason to think he would be a good provider for his family. He was well known in and around Elstow and Bedford. Wares from the Bunyan forge had been purchased by local residents for years. He was young, strong, and hardworking. He would, with diligence and thrift, do well.

The newlyweds took what few possessions they had and moved into their cottage in Elstow, a modest residence with a thatched roof and lean-to forge at its south end.[7] Beneath the roof, with its windowed-dormers, was a typical Tudor design: sturdy, practical, and unostentatious. Its brick chimney was located on the left gable end as one stood facing the house. The beams inside were crafted from English oak, and two large windows framed the substantially timbered main door.

Life for most villagers in Bedfordshire was thoroughly rural. Most, but not all, worked on land owned by the local gentry. In this, the Bunyans were fortunate. As a tradesman, he worked for himself.

Homes like the Bunyans' were heated by wood, peat, or

coal, and their main floors were made of earth. Cottage gardens were common, and housewives typically cultivated herbs and vegetables. Sometimes there were one or two fruit trees—apple and pear in most instances. During leisure time, music might be played on the lute or violin, sometimes on a hard-carved flute. Those who could read chose largely religious literature, though some drama was also read.[8]

Bearing all this in mind, a picture begins to emerge of Bunyan and his wife sitting at a table and chairs of his making in the early morning. After a breakfast of porridge and a gill of cider,[9] John gives her an affectionate kiss and strides over to the out-building housing his forge. She moves to take her seat at a spinning wheel, or perhaps goes out into the garden to tend her herbs and vegetables in the warm summer sun.

Bunyan is soon to be a first-time father, and that thought fills his mind. Walking through his workshop door, the tall and strong-boned brazier with his reddish hair, ruddy face, sparkling eyes, and rugged good looks begins stoking the fires of the forge.[10] He readies his tools for the day's work ahead. Soon the sound of a hammer striking an anvil reverberates through the morning air. It strikes a familiar rhythm—a rhythm born of long years of practice. His neighbors knew it to be the rhythm of a young man building a life for himself and his family.

THE UNEXPECTED DOWRY

Good books are true friends.

—Francis Bacon

Notwithstanding Bunyan's slender inventory of the possessions he and his wife had, she did bring something of a dowry with her: two books once owned by her father.

It seems scarcely worth noticing. But these books were to have a telling influence on Bunyan's life. This was a recurring theme. One gets the sense that, like Abraham Lincoln—a young man of modest means and keen intellectual curiosity—he savored the few books he could get his hands on. Through readings and rereadings, the cadences of an author's prose—individual lines or memorable passages—became all the more deeply ingrained because the experience of engaging ideas and insights through the written word was so relatively rare. There is every reason to think Bunyan read books with the kind of avidity and total engagement he displayed in the athletic contests he so obviously relished. Other commentators have noted this, saying he possessed a capacity to live within the books he read.[1]

It was a capacity, sad to say, more common in the seventeenth and eighteenth centuries than it is today. One hundred years and an ocean away from Bunyan's time and country, New Englanders like John and Abigail Adams also lived within the books they read. Historian David McCullough has spoken of this with eloquence and insight:

> We are what we read more than we know. And it was true no less in that distant founding time. Working on the life of John Adams, I tried to read not only what he and others of his day wrote, but what they read . . . Swift, Pope, Defoe, Sterne, Fielding, and Samuel Johnson . . . I then began to find lines from these writers turning up in the letters of my American subjects, turning up without attribution, because the lines were part of them, part of who they were and how they thought and expressed themselves.[2]

Aside from his great love of books, the rough-hewn side of Bunyan's character sometimes led him into extended periods of sowing wild oats. Still, his behavior does not appear to have been particularly egregious. It was marked most often by roisterous, rowdy behavior and coarse language—accompanied by periods of introspection about perceived immoral excess.

It is easy enough to understand. Young men put to learn

trades often develop patterns of coarse speech and conduct. That such things were common appears in the roustabout exploits of *The Tinker of Turvey*.

For Bunyan, any tendencies toward raucous behavior and crude language would have been reinforced by the roughness of military life. During his three years in the parliamentary army, he would have seen every kind of immorality common to the lot of soldiers. And while there is little evidence to suggest he took part in "illicit amours," drunken revels, looting, and the like, he certainly was exposed to people who did such things, or to regimental scuttlebutt about such behavior. The most frequent crimes among Cromwell's soldiers, for example, were swearing, drunkenness, and plundering.[3]

Punishment for such offenses was severe—administered publicly so as to have the greatest effect. In May 1655, just a few years after Bunyan's time in the army, a soldier in the regiment of a certain Colonel Axtell was found guilty of drunkenness, swearing, and quarreling. He was sentenced to three days imprisonment on bread and water. Following this, he was forced to stand with a cleft stick on his tongue for half an hour, near the door of a Mr. Henry Halfpenny (the felicitously named Covent Garden victualler in whose establishment the soldier had caused a disturbance) with a paper attached to his shirt declaring in capital letters the nature of his offenses and a notice that he was soon to be cashiered from the army.[4]

The moral offenses described in a military manual used by Cromwell's army detail other types of immorality that occurred. Among these were "rapes and ravishments," adultery, fornication, robbery and theft, murder, "the stealing of a dead man's possessions,"[5] and desertion. For such acts, punishments were meted out through fines, demotion, court-martial, imprisonment, whipping, and death.[6] Soldiers sentenced to be whipped commonly received thirty to sixty lashes.[7]

War is a hellish enterprise that brings out the best and worst in people. An impressionable young man like Bunyan would have come away from the army with some of his rough edges made rougher still.

Bunyan was only twenty or twenty-one when he married in 1649. He was still coming of age, still finding his way in the world. He was very much a young man, with the bundle of contradictions in thought and behavior that come with this stage in life.

So it was that his young wife's unexpected dowry—the two books she had inherited—began to shape his outlook on life. She began, as many a young wife has, to smooth the rough edges in her husband. Readily discerning his good qualities, she sought to draw them out. This was natural enough, as she was a religious woman, and now she sought to interest him in matters of faith.

Bunyan, for his part, began to show that he had a teachable and inquiring heart. He and his bride were compatible in many ways—particularly in their shared fondness for reading. Soon, they began to read the books she had inherited together. "My mercy," he wrote in his autobiography,

> was to light upon a Wife whose Father was counted godly: this Woman and I, though we came together as poor as poor might be . . . had for her part, *The Plain Mans Path-way to*

Heaven, and *The Practice of Piety*, which her Father had left her when he died. In these two Books I should sometimes read with her, wherein I also found some things that were somewhat pleasing to me: (but all this while I met with no conviction). She also would often tell me what a godly man her father was.... Wherefore these books... did beget within me some desires to Religion.[8]

These books, and his wife's counsel, took hold of Bunyan in a way he had not expected. He was not particularly religious, but slowly, and in ways of which he was only half aware, he began to take the measure of his heart and wrestle with the great questions about "the chief end of man."[9] So began a long spiritual quest that would transform this rough-hewn soldier with hidden depths into the pilgrim who crafted one of the great masterworks of English literature.

"A PATH THAT
SKIRTED MADNESS"

No one . . . can ever forget the impression of that
awful chapter in *Grace Abounding*, in which the
sinner takes refuge in place after place only to
expect that roof after roof will crash down upon him,
and that he is safe nowhere if the very Universe that
he inherits belongs to one who is his enemy. Nor
will anyone forget the chapter in which the sinner is
reconciled to the Universe, and walks about the
fields and cannot forbear from talking to the birds
about the great mercy of God.[1]

—G. K. Chesterton

Andrew Lang, a much-honored and scholarly son of the
heather after whom a prestigious annual lecture series
at St. Andrews University was named, was a man possessed of many gifts as a writer. His introduction to Izaak Walton's

Compleat Angler—that seventeenth-century paean to the fisher-man's art—with its pastoral images of rills and copses, is a classic of its kind. It has one of the great opening sentences in scholarly literature: self-effacing, apposite, and just. "To write on Walton," Lang confessed, "is, indeed, to hold a candle to the sun."

Lang's gifts as a prose stylist were demonstrated further when he compared Walton with John Bunyan. Both, he said, were reverent men. Both infused their works with arresting images of the English countryside and sturdy pilgrims.[2] Yet their spiritual journeys could not have been more different. Walton gloried in the Church of England. He was faithful to its authority and teaching, an apparent stranger to spiritual travail. Bunyan was a dissenter whose faith was the result of a desperate and prolonged struggle. Few men suffered a more hellish dark night of the soul than he. Lang took the measure of Bunyan's harrowing conversion narrative and penned what is perhaps the best one-sentence summary ever written about it. "Bunyan," he wrote, "could be saved only by following a path that skirted madness, and 'as by fire.'"[3]

The books written about Bunyan are legion, and nearly always, their accounts of Bunyan's conversion run to great length. Bunyan's own narrative of the mental and spiritual anguish he suffered runs to such length and reels so often from near solace to despair that it is often difficult to step back and see the larger picture. The reader is drawn in so thoroughly that it is difficult to struggle free of Bunyan's self-described slough of despond. C. S. Lewis captured this dilemma memorably in his brief summary of Bunyan's autobiography. "*Grace Abounding*," he stated, "is a nightmare—you can't lay it down—and you can't forget it. But its fascination is not that of art. The pity and terror we feel aren't those of tragedy. It's more as if we'd visited an asylum."[4]

The length of time assigned to Bunyan's gradual spiritual transformation has varied among the scholarly community. Some, including the most recent editors of Bunyan's autobiography, *Grace Abounding*, feel it lasted for six years, from 1649 to 1655.[5] Some feel it lasted for four years, from 1650 to 1654.[6] Still others feel it lasted just under three years, beginning in 1650.[7]

Regardless of the chronology, Bunyan's spiritual transformation was the seminal event of his life. Had it not taken place in the way that it did, *The Pilgrim's Progress* might never have been written.

One of the most painstaking efforts to fix a chronology for this transformation was undertaken by Bunyan scholar Richard Greaves in his magisterial study, *Glimpses of Glory: John Bunyan and English Dissent*. Utilizing the internal evidence provided in *Grace Abounding*, he determined the year in which Bunyan's transformation commenced as 1650. It was not fully complete, he felt, until late 1657 or early 1658, meaning that the transformation lasted between seven and eight years all told.[8]

C. S. Lewis stated that reading *Grace Abounding* was like visiting an asylum.[9] This is a key insight, and one with which Bunyan scholar Richard Greaves seems to agree. He wrote that Bunyan's transformation was psychological as well as spiritual. It could not, therefore, be complete until it was clear that Bunyan had reached a place of lasting peace—peace of mind as well as a sense of spiritual peace.

In *Grace Abounding*, Bunyan referred to a time of spiritual awakening. It began in 1650, the year in which his blind daughter Mary was born.[10] Prior to this, he had been reading the two books his wife had inherited from her father, *The Practice of Piety* and *The Plain Man's Pathway to Heaven*. They were an important early influence; but in the end, they only produced a cursory interest in spiritual things and a self-satisfied, outward conformity to high-church ceremonies.[11] As Bunyan recalled:

> Wherefore these books . . . though they did not reach my heart to awaken it . . . yet they did beget within me some desires to Religion . . . [I would] go to Church twice a day, and . . . very devoutly both say and sing as others did; yet retaining my wicked life: but withal, I was so overrun with the spirit of superstition, that I adored, and that with great devotion, even all things (both the High-place, Priest, Clerk, Vestments, Service, and what else) belonging to the Church.[12]

This period of outward conformity lasted for about a year (from 1649 to 1650). But aside from his reading of the books his wife had inherited, and her counsel about the godly example of her father, there were other inducements.[13]

The first of these was a sermon on Sabbath observance that prompted a deep sense of reflection within Bunyan, tinged with feelings of guilt over the team sports he loved and the work he had occasionally performed on the Sabbath. He long remembered the moment:

I fell in my conscience under his sermon, thinking and believing that he made that sermon on purpose to show me my evil doing . . . [A]t that time I felt what guilt was, though never before, that I can remember; [I] went home when the sermon was ended, with a great burden upon my spirit.[14]

But these feelings, however much Bunyan remembered them in retrospect, passed within a matter of hours. They had cast a pall over what he called his "best delights"[15] that recalls Eric Liddell's dilemma in *Chariots of Fire*. But unlike Liddell, Bunyan fought free of the misgivings he felt almost before he had his Sunday dinner. "Before I well dined," he wrote, "the trouble began to go off my minde . . . [M]y heart returned to its old course . . . I shook the Sermon out of my mind, and [returned] to my old custom of sports and gaming . . . with great delight."[16]

To the modern ear, it seems strange that any sense of guilt would attach itself to a habit of playing sports on Sunday. Few things seem more harmless than pickup games of football after church—to cite one example—where one can enjoy the camaraderie of friends often known from childhood. But Bunyan's time was one when religion dominated a man's daily life in ways that are alien to us now. The Anglican faith was the state religion. Even if one was not particularly religious, attendance at Sunday services was compulsory, as was tithing. From baptism, schooling, and marriage to one's funeral and burial, the church was omnipresent. Week in and week out, from cradle to grave, its pervasive influence was felt.

Bunyan was a man of spirit—a gifted athlete who, it is not

too much to say, cherished sport. But he had hidden depths as well, sensitivities and sensibilities in keeping with an artistic nature. As we learned in an earlier chapter, as a boy he had also had disturbing and terrifying childhood dreams of fiends and hellfire—he had heard voices and seen visions—that were a torment to him. Those memories had been dormant for many years, but one can see how a powerful or luridly presented sermon on breaking the Sabbath might have brought them to the surface.

This, it seems, is exactly what happened. For while Bunyan believed he had almost immediately shaken off the guilt prompted by the Sabbath sermon, he hadn't really. The very same day he had felt and fought free of it, he joined his friends for a game of tipcat. When his second turn to bat came, he was prepared to do as he did for his first time: strike the small billet of wood, or "cat," with his cudgel. But all at once he had a vision of Christ "looking down upon me . . . very hotly displeased."[17]

Was it a "road to Damascus" event, or a resurfacing of deeply troubling memories? It seems to have been a mingling of both. Bunyan clearly believed he had seen a vision. But he also wrote that within this visionary moment he felt his heart "sink in despair."[18] This was unnerving, and he did not know how to deal with it. Having resolved to not confide in anyone, he "returned desperately to [his] sport again."[19] He would not let these dark misgivings get the better of him. But despair seized him as with a giant's strength. He could not escape its grasp, and he felt himself to be damned.

Before so formidable an enemy, Bunyan could only fall back. He had persuaded himself he was damned; and however incredible such a thing seems, that was his reality. He had reached a place known to the writer of Ecclesiastes, who "commended mirth, because a man hath no better thing under the sun, than to eat, and to drink, and to be merry."[20]

He continued desperate and despairing for a month or more. Then one day, while standing before a neighbor's shop window, he found himself "cursing, swearing, and playing the Mad-man, after my wonted manner."[21] One can well imagine that after several years' service in the army, Bunyan could turn the air blue when the mood took him.

The shopkeeper's wife overheard him, and while she was neither religious nor prudish, she came out to where Bunyan was and let loose a fusillade of scorn and reproach. "She told me," Bunyan recalled, "that I was the ungodliest fellow for swearing that ever she heard in all her life; and that I [would] spoil all the youth in a whole town, if they came . . . in my company. At this reproof I was silenced, and put to secret shame."[22]

Shamed and surprisingly repentant, Bunyan immediately ceased to curse and swear as he had done. In the days that followed, his neighbors were astonished by the marked alteration in his behavior. Not long afterward, he met a man "who . . . did talk pleasantly of the Scriptures." This appealed to him, and he "began to take great pleasure" in reading his Bible. He found himself drawn to the Ten Commandments, the careful observance of which, he thought, could furnish "my way to Heaven." For "about a twelve-month," he later recalled, "I thought I pleased God as well as any man in England."[23]

All of the aforementioned events unfolded in the year following Bunyan's marriage in 1649. It was after all of these things, sometime in 1650, that his spiritual awakening commenced. All that happened heretofore was by way of prelude—a setting of the stage.

The story was this. One day, Bunyan's trade took him to Bedford, where he happened upon "three or four poor women sitting at a door in the sun, and talking about the things of God." Curious, he drew closer. He listened for a while, but then he found himself puzzled. "I heard, but I understood not," he remembered,

> for their talk was about a new birth [and] the work of God on their hearts . . . they talked how God had visited their souls with His love in the Lord Jesus, and with what words and promises they had been refreshed, comforted, and supported against the temptations of the Devil . . . and how they were borne up under his assaults . . . they spake as if joy did make them speak; they spake with such pleasantness of Scripture language, and with such appearance of grace in all they said, that they were to me as if they had found a new world.[24]

This was seed that fell on good ground. These women spoke of refreshment, solace, and strength in the face of such things. Could this be true? Could he really be set free from fears that had never left him? It was as if a lifeline had been thrown to a drowning man.

Bunyan found himself lost in reflection and thought, but of a different kind than he had experienced previously. His reflections were now imbued with hope. As he wrote: "[After] I had heard and considered what [the women had] said, I left them, and went about my employment again: but their talk and discourse went with me; also my heart would tarry with them, for I was greatly affected with their words."[25]

Bunyan resolved to seek out people like the women he had heard. In a short time, this brought him to the congregation of John Gifford. Bunyan had discovered within himself "a great softness and tenderness of heart." As he listened to Gifford's descriptions of the new birth, he felt "a great bending in my mind to a continual meditating on it." The process of his true spiritual awakening had begun.[26]

THE COMING OF
EVANGELIST

We took sweet counsel together, and walked unto
the house of God in company.

—Psalm 55:14 KJV

John Gifford was a remarkable man, "as little likely"—to quote John Brown—to do what he did "as was Saul of Tarsus to become Paul the Apostle."[1] Bunyan's friendship with him was no less striking. He became Bunyan's spiritual mentor, and it was he upon whom the character of Evangelist in *The Pilgrim's Progress* was based.

Gifford's story is fascinating. A native of Kent, at the outbreak of the civil war he was a royalist and a major in the king's army. In 1648, one more desperate struggle took place in Kent to win back the country for the king. Near the end of May, Gifford took part in the fiercest part of the uprising—a pitched battle that began about a mile outside Maidstone with hand-to-hand fighting and ended in town. It was reported,

> that victory was declared for [the parliamentary forces of Lord General] Fairfax, the [royalist] insurgents leaving 300 of their number dead in the streets . . . 1,400 surrendered as prisoners, some of them being taken in the early morning as they were hiding in the woods, hop-gardens, and fields round the town. Among these prisoners was John Gifford.

The vast majority of the royalists who surrendered were to be released. Gifford and eleven others were sentenced to be hanged.[2]

Then Gifford's story took a twist. On the night before he was to die, his sister came to visit him. She gained admittance and discovered that several of the sentinels who guarded her brother were either drunk or asleep. She told her brother of this, and the two quietly slipped away.

Once outside the prison, Gifford crept into a well-hidden ditch in a nearby field—perhaps one overgrown by an impenetrable hedgerow. He remained there for three days, until the great search for him had ceased. With the help of royalist friends, he was taken to London in disguise. After a brief stay, he escaped into the countryside, moving at intervals from safe house to safe house. Arriving at last in Bedford, where he was unknown, he declared himself to be a doctor and began to practice medicine. As a major who had formerly served in the royalist army, he had probably acquired enough rudimentary knowledge of battlefield medicine to carry this deception off.

Gifford had made good his escape. But rather than settle down to a quiet, unobtrusive existence, he began to drink and gamble heavily. He often lost, and his losses soon mounted. One evening, he lost the then-considerable sum of fifteen pounds.[3] He became enraged and "thought many desperate thoughts against God."[4]

It was then that Gifford had an Augustinian "take up and read" experience. Somehow, he acquired and read a book written by the Puritan writer Robert Bolton—perhaps Bolton's *Treatise on Comforting Afflicted Consciences*. Whatever the book's title was, Bolton had been a man much like Gifford, and had experienced a dramatic conversion.

Gifford now came under great conviction, undergoing a spiritual transformation that lasted for a month or more. At its close, he had a profound sense that he had received "forgiveness of his sins for the sake of Christ." He only lived for another five years, but in that time he became the unlikely pastor of the nonconformist church in Bedford—the church John Bunyan began attending.

It was a most extraordinary turn of events. Bunyan had served in the parliamentary army; Gifford was a royalist officer. As former soldiers on opposite sides of a war that had savaged Britain, both bore about them scars that were among the most difficult to heal.

But the beguiling grace that had transformed Gifford's life contrived to bring them together. It proved a bridge both could cross to forge an unlikely and deeply important friendship. Bunyan had need of a counselor like Gifford. For as his awakening progressed into the long and gradual conversion it became, he experienced many storms and difficulties. True, he was formally received into the church at Bedford in 1653 while still living in Elstow, and baptized in 1655 when he and his family moved there. Without question, these were signs of real progress. But a true and enduring sense of peace proved maddeningly elusive. Thankfully, at least for a time, Gifford was there to help him find his way.

Bunyan began attending the Bedford church in 1653, the same year Gifford entered into residence as its minister. Sadly, Gifford died in early September 1655, leaving only about two years for Bunyan to benefit from his pastoral counsel.

Following a close study of church records and other surviving manuscripts, John Brown reported that Gifford was "a man of sufficient force of character to be capable of impressing powerfully men who were themselves of strong individuality."[5] After he had met Gifford, Bunyan began to experience firsthand "the soul-subduing power of this converted Royalist major."[6] Gifford, Bunyan recalled, "took occasion to talk with me, and was willing to be well-persuaded of me. . . . [H]e invited me to his House, where I should hear him confer with others about the dealings of God with the Soul."[7] Still later, in *Grace Abounding*, Bunyan wrote: "I sat under the ministry of holy Mr. Gifford, whose Doctrine, by God's Grace, was much for my stability."

Bunyan did not gain a lasting stability, or peace, until some two years after Gifford's death. But that there was any stability at all during the stormy periods of his conversion was owing not a little to the extraordinary man whom he would later immortalize as Evangelist.

Navigating the nightmare that C. S. Lewis called Bunyan's *Grace Abounding* is a difficult task at best. At times Bunyan thought himself within sight of the shores of grace; at others he was convinced he had committed the unpardonable sin and was irretrievably damned. Morbid fancies seized him. He imagined that the apostles Peter, Paul, and John, indeed all the writers of Scripture, "did look with scorn upon me, and hold me in derision; and as if they said unto me, 'All our words are truth . . . It is not we that have cut you off, but you have cast away yourself.'"[8]

Hellish temptations beset him as well. The following account is as representative as any of the depths to which he descended: "Thus, by the strange and unusual assaults of the tempter, was my soul, like a broken vessel, driven as with the winds, and tossed sometimes headlong into despair."[9] At other times, haunting images competed with one another to convey how utterly destitute Bunyan felt. He saw himself "as a house whose foundations are destroyed," or "as a drowning child in a mill-pond." And so the awful conflict continued. Days and weeks passed, during which he was "sometimes comforted, and sometimes tormented."[10]

In the period between John Gifford's death in September 1655 and the resolution of Bunyan's spiritual turmoil in late 1657 or early 1658, Bunyan suffered still more.[11] He developed worrying symptoms of consumption.[12] "I was," he wrote, "suddenly and violently seized with much weakness . . . insomuch that I thought I could not live."[13] The lament that followed sounds as though it were written by Job. "Now my sickness was doubled upon me."[14]

How long Bunyan's consumptive symptoms lingered is not known. But near the end of his illness, his spiritual turmoil finally ended. One evening, as he sat by the fire, he had an epiphany: "I suddenly felt this word to sound in my heart, 'I must go to Jesus.' . . . At this my former darkness . . . fled away, and the blessed things of heaven were set within my view."

Then followed a poignant and all too rare glimpse into the life Bunyan shared with his family in the cottage on St. Cuthbert's Street. The scene he described was an unfolding of how mercy found him at the last. Overtaken by a sudden sense of joy and peace, he turned to his wife as they sat before their fireplace and said, "Wife, is there ever such a scripture, 'I must go to Jesus?'"

Perhaps looking up from some knitting, she said she wasn't sure—in that way that wives have said to husbands from time immemorial. Bunyan fell to musing. A few minutes later his thoughts were drawn to a passage from the New Testament book of Hebrews:

> Ye are come unto mount Sion, and unto the City of the living God, the heavenly Jerusalem, and to an innumerable company of Angels . . . to God the Judge of all, and to the spirits of just men made perfect, and to Jesus the Mediator of the New Testament, and to the blood of sprinkling, that speaketh better things than that of Abel.[15]

It was for him a "blessed sentence"—a passage that led him to another verse and then to still more. The words in each place to which he turned seemed words of comfort and tranquility.

"The Lord led me," he said, "and showed me wonderful glory in every one of them." Even from the distance of years, he could always recall how he then felt: "These words . . . have oft since this time been great refreshment to my spirit. Blessed be God in having mercy on me."[16]

"That night," he remembered, "was a good night to me . . . I could scarce lie in my bed for joy, and peace, and triumph."[17] The memory of these feelings later formed the basis of one of the most cherished passages from *The Pilgrim's Progress*:

Up this way therefore did burdened Christian run, but not without great difficulty, because of the load on his back.

He ran thus till he came at a place somewhat ascending; and upon that place stood a Cross, and a little below, in the bottom a Sepulchre. So I saw in my dream, that just as Christian came up with the Cross, his burden loosed from off his shoulders, and fell from off his back, and began to tumble, and so continued to do till it came to the mouth of the Sepulchre, where it fell in, and I saw it no more.

Then was Christian glad and lightsome, and said, with a merry heart, "He hath given me rest by His sorrow, and life by His death." Then he stood awhile to look and wonder, for it was very surprising to him, that the sight of the Cross should thus ease him of his burden. He looked therefore, and looked again, even till the springs that were in his head sent the waters down his cheeks . . . Now, as he stood looking and weeping, behold three Shining Ones came to him and saluted him with "Peace be to thee." So the first said to him, "Thy sins be forgiven thee" . . . the second stripped him of his rags, and clothed him with change of raiment; the third also set a mark on his forehead, and gave him a roll with a seal upon it . . . that he should give it in at the Celestial Gate . . .

Then Christian gave three leaps for joy, and went on singing:

> *Thus far I did come laden with my sin;*
> *Nor could aught ease the grief that I was in,*
> *Till I came hither: What a place is this!*
> *Must here be the beginning of my bliss?*
> *Must here the burden fall from off my back?*
> *Must here the strings that bound it to me crack?*
> *Blest Cross! blest Sepulchre! blest, rather, be*
> *The Man that there was put to shame for me!*[18]

A MENDER OF SOULS

I preached as never sure to preach again, And as
a dying man to dying men.[1]

—Richard Baxter

For some time before he finally struggled free of his own slough of despond, Bunyan had been preaching. It had begun innocently enough, when in 1655 he was asked to "speak a word of exhortation"——or word of encouragement——to the members of the Bedford church he had joined recently. Like many a first-time speaker in a church setting, he was hesitant. Yet he and those who heard him soon discovered that he had a gift.

Bunyan's gifts as a writer reveal that he had a ready wit and could tell a good story. He was tall and good-looking, and so had a "pulpit presence" that was impressive. His genuine regard for people was winsome, and this commended him to church-goers, as surviving recollections of his ministry attest.

Not all of these gifts and strengths were present when Bunyan first began to preach. But he found his feet quickly— and his audiences responded warmly. Surviving accounts reveal that people felt themselves to be "affected and comforted" when he spoke. In a phrase, he could "bring people along with him." In fact, he had been bringing people along with him right from the start, when in 1653 he first began traveling from Elstow to attend the Bedford church. "When I went out," Bunyan wrote,

> to seek the Bread of Life [in Bedford], some of them would follow me and the rest be put into a muse at home. Yea, almost all the town at first at times would go out to hear at the place where I found good. Yea, young and old for a while had some reformation on them; also, some of them perceiving that God had mercy on me, came crying to Him for mercy too.[2]

John Gifford must have wondered what he had on his hands when Bunyan and what amounted to a small entourage from Elstow started attending his services. This brazier-turned-seeker was no ordinary new parishioner.[3] Gifford must have seen a bit of himself as well in Bunyan: a former soldier, a bit rough around the edges—but with undoubted gifts and potential. Intelligence, wit, charm, a concern for others, and an artless sincerity—all these things were written in his character.

John Brown wrote that Bunyan's preaching was distinguished by an obvious desire "to win the homage of men's hearts."[4] There was something disarming about a man who could give himself wholly to what he said and urged upon his hearers. This stood in stark contrast to the formal, often-turgid addresses given to Church of England congregations. Bunyan's sermons, it was said, were marked by clarity and freedom of speech. He used parables and homely illustrations to describe spiritual truths in a way that lingered in the memory. Then, too, there was a power to his address. At times Bunyan testified to the feeling that he spoke "as if an Angel were at his back."[5] Taking these things into account, one can see why those who heard him responded warmly.

Other memories of Bunyan's ministry have survived. If strong biographical traditions are to be believed, his career was colorful and not without its adventures. John Brown wrote:

> the author of the little sketch of [Bunyan's] life published in 1700, also tells us that he, "being to preach in a country village in Cambridgeshire" . . . a Cambridge scholar, and none of the soberest of them neither, enquired what was the meaning of that concourse of people . . . [When] told that one Bunyan, a tinker, was to preach there, he gave a boy two-pence to hold his horse, saying, 'He was resolved to hear the tinker prate,' and so he went into the church to hear him.[6]

Another story from the pre-restoration years concerns Bunyan's encounter on the road near Cambridge with another university man, who asked him how he, not having the original Scriptures, dared to preach. Bunyan was nothing if not quick on his feet, and so he answered the scholar with a question: "Do you, sir, have the originals—the actual copies of the books written by the prophets and apostles?"

"No," the scholar replied, "but I have what I know to be true copies of the originals."

Perhaps there was the hint of a smile in Bunyan's reply. "And I," he said, "believe the English Bible to be a true copy also." At a loss for words, the university man turned and went on his way.[7]

Still another story describes the kind of settings in which Bunyan preached, and the opponents he sometimes encountered. It seems that a man named Daniel Angier, of Toft, in Cambridgeshire, occasionally invited Bunyan to come and preach in his barn. In May 1659, Bunyan was holding a service in Angier's barn, when toward the end of the sermon in walked Thomas Smith of Cambridge, a redoubtable man who was rector of Gawcat, a professor of Arabic, reader in rhetoric, lecturer at Christ's College, and keeper of the university library.[8]

Bunyan was preaching from 1 Timothy 4:16, which reads: "Pay close attention to yourself and to your teaching; persevere in these things, for as you do this you will ensure salvation both for yourself and for those who hear you" (NASB).

In the course of his sermon, Bunyan expressed a concern that most among his audience were unbelievers. At the close of the service, Smith confronted him, asking, "What right have you to say that men, half of whose faces you've never seen before, are unbelievers? Did not St. Paul call the people to whom he wrote 'saints and beloved of God'? Do not all the Protestant preachers overseas address those who hear them as *Fideles*? What right have you, then, to call a company of baptized people unbelievers?" These questions were tantamount to saying: "You, sir, are uncharitable. And being uncharitable, you are unfit to preach."

To this Bunyan replied that when Christ preached from a ship to people on the shore, he taught that there were four kinds of ground into which the good seed of the sower fell, and that only one of the four brought forth fruit. "Now," said Bunyan, "if your position is to be believed, Christ had no charity and was not fit to preach the gospel."[9]

After Bunyan had thus defended himself, his friend Daniel Angier rose to rebuke Smith. In reply, Smith denied Bunyan's right to preach, asking, "What have you to say to the apostle's question: 'How shall they preach except they be sent?'"

To this Bunyan understandably replied that the church at Bedford had sent him. Smith shot back, saying that the church at Bedford, being comprised of lay people, could not give Bunyan, a mere tinker, authority which they themselves did not have. At this, he turned and left the barn.[10]

But this was not the end of the matter—not, at least, so far as Smith was concerned. Several weeks later he published "A Letter to Mr. E. of Taft [sic], four miles from Cambridge." In this pamphlet Smith tried the mud-slinging polemic approach, hoping that most if not all of what was thrown would stick to the rhetorical wall. He charged Bunyan with unseemly presumption, if not illegality in taking it upon himself to preach. And if such preaching was not illegal, it was certainly sinful—so say nothing of his belief that Bunyan was guilty on several counts of spreading false doctrine.

The close of Smith's pamphlet was marked by condemnation and baseless allegation. "If any man among you," he wrote, "though he be a wandering preaching tinker . . . seemeth to be religious, and bridleth not his tongue, that man's religion is vain." Bunyan, he said, had done violence by intruding into a parish and causing the people of Toft "to hate their lawful minister (John Ellis)." Worst of all, Smith charged Bunyan (to whom he kept referring derisively as "the tinker") with encouraging those who heard him in Angier's barn "to cudgel [Ellis] and break open the church doors by violence."[11]

Bunyan did not reply to Smith's letter in print. However, a Cambridge man named Henry Denne now took up Bunyan's defense. As it happened, Denne was an old friend of Smith, so there was no small measure of irony in play. Denne said to Smith:

> You seem to be angry with the tinker because he strives to mend souls as well as kettles and pans . . . Give me leave to propound something for your consideration: Some shipwrackt men, swimming to an island, find there many inhabitants, to whom they preach; the heathen hearing are converted, and walk together in love, praising the Lord: [Tell me, was] the preaching of these shipwrackt men a sin? Secondly, [is it] not lawful for this congregation [at Bedford] to chuse to themselves pastors, governours, teachers, &c.? Thirdly, [may not] this congregation may not find some fitting men full of faith and the Holy Ghost to preach to other unbelieving heathen?[12]

There must have been more than a little gnashing of teeth when Smith read Denne's staunch and unexpected defense of "the tinker from Bedford." And to be sure, the stories recounted above are entertaining. They furnish a unique glimpse of Bunyan's personality and pastoral ministry.

Still, it must be said that however much of a stir Bunyan made as a fledgling preacher, he labored as a wounded soldier. As the previous chapter has shown, he was subject to intense and prolonged periods of depression and despair. This seems to suggest that he suffered from a chronic psychiatric condition known as dysthemia[13]—a mood disorder marked by symptoms that include poor appetite, insomnia, listlessness, low self-esteem, and feelings of hopelessness.[14]

Bunyan was in this sense a study in contradictions. He felt drawn to the consolations of the gospel, yet a full and lasting sense of those consolations eluded him for several years. He felt impelled to tell others that there was hope for them in Christ, yet he sometimes felt a debilitating sense of hopelessness. Notwithstanding, such hope as he had found or could point to, he wished to share with others.

That Bunyan had obvious gifts as a preacher was undeniable; and this was recognized in 1655 when the Bedford church formally commissioned him for the task of public preaching.[15] But it was equally undeniable that Bunyan's life experiences were those of a man who endured great hardship and tragedy in the early years of his preaching ministry. "Almost from the time of his removal from Elstow to Bedford," John Brown wrote, "Bunyan's life seems to have been darkened by sorrow."[16] The symptoms of consumption that he developed occurred at this time—likely brought on by an "intense overstrain of mind and heart."[17]

But mental and physical illness were not all that Bunyan had to contend with in these years. In 1658 his wife died. "A dark shadow," it was said, "came over his home and clouded his heart and life. He was spared, but the wife of his youth was taken. Under the shadow of this great bereavement, Bunyan was still battling with inward conflict; but he had at the same time to be both father and mother to his poor blind child and to the other three children whom his wife had, in dying, left to his care."[18]

Still grieving, Bunyan had to confront the pressing practical need of finding a new wife to help him raise his children. He could not do it alone. In this case necessity and solace converged. In a matter of months he met and married his "well-beloved wife Elizabeth."[19] After all that he had come through, he had found an unlooked-for mercy.

"NO ORDINARY
DIFFICULTIES"[1]

Except for the peculiar tumult of the mid-
seventeenth century, the world might never have
heard of John Bunyan.[2]

—Ola Winslow

The year that unfolded between November 1659 and
November 1660—one hundred years before Britain's
celebrated *annus mirabilis*, or year of wonders—was
anything but that for John Bunyan, or, indeed, Britain itself.

At the outset, one would have thought otherwise. Bunyan,
the father of four children and a widower for approximately
one year, had met and married his second wife, Elizabeth. Her
conduct in later life revealed qualities that doubtless attracted
Bunyan to her. She was a devoted, caring, and steadfast woman.
She was also willing to assume a daunting task: becoming a

stepmother to four children who were not her own. It must have been a great comfort for John Bunyan to know that he had found a bride who could love him and his children. Nine-year-old Mary, especially, blind from birth, would continue to require special care. This Elizabeth promised to give, as she would do her best to help raise Mary's siblings, Elizabeth, John, and Thomas.[3]

Bunyan's domestic happiness notwithstanding, storm clouds had gathered anew on the political horizon. On May 25, 1659, Richard Cromwell, Oliver's hapless, indecisive son, abdicated as Lord Protector of England. He had only one other claim to fame. When he died fifty-three years later, he was, in terms of his age, the longest-lived ruler or former ruler of England.[4] It was a dubious distinction.

After Richard Cromwell's fall from power, a royalist rebellion led by Sir George Booth commenced. It was defeated on August 19 by parliamentary forces under Major-General John Lambert at the battle of Winnington Bridge near Northwich. This showed how real the threat of renewed civil war was.[5] If an all-out civil war had broken out, it would have been the third such conflict in Bunyan's lifetime.

The Long Parliament that brought the Cromwells into power met its demise at about the same time. A new and predominantly royalist Parliament was elected in its place. Within a matter of months, in May 1660, Charles II resumed the throne his father had lost. The period known as the Restoration had begun.

For some time before Charles's return, Bunyan and the Bedford congregation had been much in prayer over national events. They expected a return of dark days for dissenters like themselves, but they had no way of knowing how soon they would suffer a great loss. John Gifford's successor as their pastor, John Burton, died in September 1660. In addition to everything else, they were now without a minister.

But worse was to come. Almost as soon as Charles resumed the throne, a crackdown on religious dissent began. In early November, Bunyan was arrested for having transgressed a long-unenforced Elizabethan act against conventicles (secret or illegal religious meetings) and nonconformity with the Church of England. Instead of confining his preaching to private visits with people in their homes, which was permitted, he had continued to hold public meetings. It was a principled act of defiance against policies he felt to be unjust.[6]

According to biographer John Brown, on November 12, 1660, Bunyan saddled his horse and rode over to the little hamlet of Lower Samsell, by Harlington, about thirteen miles to the south of Bedford.[7] The village was situated in a finely wooded, undulating country.

Bunyan's errand was an appointment he had promised to keep: to hold a religious service in a farmhouse belonging to a fellow dissenter. Riding through the thick stand of elm trees that ringed the field where the farmhouse was, he could see the lights within.

He arrived to a subdued reception. Those who were already gathered exchanged anxious looks. They told him that the neighboring magistrate, Francis Wingate, had issued a warrant for his arrest. The owner of the house approached him, saying that perhaps it would be best not to hold the meeting. He ought to make good his escape, for men were on their way to apprehend him. Bunyan penned his own account of what happened next:

> By no means I will not stir, neither will I have the meeting dismissed . . . Come, be of good cheer, let us not be daunted; our cause is good, we need not be ashamed of it; to preach God's Word is so good a work, that we shall be well rewarded, if we suffer.[8]

Following this, since there was some time yet before his service had been scheduled to start, Bunyan went outside and walked in the field by which the house was surrounded. Strolling beneath leafless branches, he felt the burden of a grave responsibility.[9]

> [It] came into my mind, that I had showed myself hearty and courageous in my preaching, and had, blessed be Grace, made it my business to encourage others; therefore, thought I, if I should now run, and make an escape, it [would] be of a very ill savour in the country. For what [would] my weak and newly converted brethren think [if] I was not so strong in deed as I was in word?[10]

Bunyan had another fear. If God in his mercy had chosen him for a forlorn hope—that he should be the first to be opposed for the gospel, and he fled—it might well be a fatal discouragement to all who might in the future face imprisonment or worse—as he now did. And what of people outside the dissenting community, or those who were unbelievers? Should he flee, would they not take occasion to disparage or blaspheme the gospel, and suspect worse of him and his Christian profession than it deserved?[11]

No, he decided, there was more at stake than his personal well-being. He turned and went back into the farmhouse. As he went in, he could see people approaching from surrounding villages: Higher Samsell and Pulloxhill on one side, Westoning and Flitwick on the other. He felt the weight of his responsibility to them. Once everyone had arrived, he called the meeting to order and opened with prayer.

We do not know what he prayed, but it must have been moving. He, and those who heard him pray, did not know how this night would end. Doubtless he prayed they would all have strength to stand. Few prayers would have closed with a more fervent amen.

Bunyan then asked them to open their Bibles, following which he began to speak. It was then the authorities burst in, ordering him to stop. They demanded to know if he and his followers had any weapons (as they were under suspicion of harboring anti-royalist sympathies). No, Bunyan replied, they had no weapons; they had met merely to speak of the truths contained in God's Word. No matter, the arresting officer said, they were going to take him away.

Bowing to the inevitable, Bunyan must have asked them to wait a moment, for he recorded what his parting words to the little congregation were:

I spake some few words of counsel and encouragement to the people, declaring to them, that they saw we were prevented of our opportunity to speak and hear the Word of God, and were like to suffer for the same . . . [I told them] they should not be discouraged, for it was a mercy to suffer upon so good account. For we might have been apprehended as thieves or murderers, or for other wickedness; but blessed be God it was not so, but we [were to] suffer as Christians for well doing: and [it was] better [we were] the persecuted than the persecutors.[12]

We do not know if Bunyan's wife and children were present, but it can only be imagined what his thoughts were as he was taken away. Elizabeth was expecting their first child. If she and his children were home asleep in their cottage in Bedford, who would bring them the news of his arrest? How on earth would they carry on?

These were questions for which he had no answers. He could only breathe a silent prayer, commending them, as he did himself, to God's care and keeping. He did not know what tomorrow would bring.

PRISONER OF
CONSCIENCE

Into this age Bunyan was thrown; a great pearl, sunk
in deep and troubled waters.[1]

—George Barrell Cheever

Bunyan was thirty-two when he was imprisoned in the
Bedford county gaol. He would remain there for the
next twelve years. His blind daughter, Mary, was ten
when he was arrested, twenty-two when he was released. His
daughter Elizabeth, age six, would turn eighteen in 1672. Upon
his release, his sons John and Thomas would have just entered
their teens or be about to do so. His daughters would have some
memory of him. His sons' memories would be hazy at best, or
nonexistent.

The extent of what Bunyan's newlywed wife, Elizabeth,
suffered is lost to history. We have scant record of her feelings

when her husband was seized, only the sad fact that the shock of this news induced a miscarriage. Awaiting trial, her husband's fate had yet to be decided; but she, and he, knew the double grief of separation from each other and a heart-wrenching loss.

It was not immediately clear what Bunyan's fate would be. For two months before his case came to trial, he remained in the Bedford county gaol. Then, early in January 1661, the quarter Sessions under which his case would be heard were convened.[2]

His trial began with a reading of the indictment against him. It was charged that he had "devilishly and perniciously abstained from coming to church to hear divine service"—that is to say, he had refused to attend services of the Church of England in Bedford—and further, that he was "a common upholder of several unlawful meetings and conventicles, to the great disturbance and distraction of the good subjects of this kingdom."[3] The indictment was based on an Elizabethan statute from 1593, which had been drawn up against "seditious sectaries and disloyal people."[4]

Once the indictment had been read out, the Sessions clerk asked Bunyan if he had anything to say. Bunyan answered that he "did go to the church of God," of which he was "by grace a member with the people over whom Christ is the head." At this, Sir John Kelynge, the chairman of the Sessions, grew impatient and asked Bunyan directly, "But do you come to church—you know what I mean—to the parish church, to hear divine service?" Bunyan replied that he did not.[5]

Bunyan could not have come before a less fair-minded man than Kelynge. Long after his death, he was remembered as "a man of evil temper"[6]—violent and overbearing—as when he fined a jury a hundred marks apiece for acquitting several poor townspeople who had met for worship with Bibles but without prayer books.[7]

Kelynge was also a blustering coward. In 1663 he was made a Judge of King's Bench, and two years later became Lord Chief Justice. The power went to his head. His conduct on the bench became arbitrary and abusive. Hauled before the House of Commons, he was severely censured and avoided a dire fate only by begging and fawning with an obsequiousness many found disgusting. Still, he failed to mend his ways. In 1670 he was compelled to humble himself at the bar of the House of Lords for his insolence to Lord Hollis on his trial in the Court of King's Bench. "Such was the man," John Brown wrote, "who presided at Bunyan's examination in 1661, and the man whom Bunyan probably had in his mind when he drew the character of Lord Hategood in the trial of Faithful at Vanity Fair."[8]

During this trial, Kelynge and Bunyan had a long inter-rogatory exchange that centered on issues of authority. Bunyan rejected the Book of Common Prayer as an unnecessary and offensive addition to Scripture written by men. Kelynge said he must abide by it. Frustrated by Bunyan's spirited defense, Kelynge returned to the indictment read out against him. Did he, Kelynge asked, acknowledge the truth of the charges made in it? Bunyan refused to say anything other than he and his friends had met often to pray and exhort one another. At such times, he said, they had enjoyed God's comforting presence.

Kelynge had heard enough. He called Bunyan a "canting pedlar" and sentenced him to three months in prison.[9] Once this sentence was served, he would either agree to attend services in the Church of England or be banished from the country. If he were banished and tried to return without the permission of the king, he would be hung. Bunyan remained defiant, saying that even if he were to be set free immediately, he would preach the following day. At this, the gavel descended and he was taken away to the Bedford county gaol.[10]

Bunyan expected to be set free at the end of his three-month sentence in the spring of 1661, but he wasn't. In a travesty of justice, no further indictment or sentence was brought against him. And in direct contravention of Habeas Corpus, he continued to be held prisoner. Uncowed, he still held to his purpose. He consistently defended the meetings in which he had taken part. All he and his friends had wished, he said, "was simply to do each other as much good as they could according to their light, and not to disturb the peace of the nation."[11] But such words continued to fall on deaf ears.

Bunyan's allegiance to principle was heroic; but his wife, Elizabeth, was no less noble or longsuffering. Indeed, there are two heroes to the backstory surrounding *The Pilgrim's Progress*. Each played their part, and Bunyan never forgot what his wife did for him.

When no one else raised a voice in Bunyan's defense, Elizabeth—young and newly married peasant girl that she was—took up his case at the Midsummer Assize of 1661. When her husband sought a hearing in open court, on three occasions she presented a petition to an assize judge requesting this. She went first to Sir Matthew Hale, who was in Bedford that year on circuit. He received her and her petition kindly, telling her he would do what good he could. Still, he feared it would be but little.[12]

The next day, as the assize judge's carriage was passing

through Bedford near St. Paul's Square, Elizabeth quickly handed a petition through the window to Thomas Twisden, who was the other assize judge. He caught it up angrily, glanced at it, and told her dismissively that it would be of no use. "Your husband cannot be released," he said, "until he promises not to preach."[13]

But Elizabeth would not accept this. She resolved to seek out Sir Matthew Hale once more. She thought him a Christian man with a generous heart. She felt certain he would help her if he could.

Elizabeth's opportunity came during a pause in the business of the court. She pushed her way toward the bench through a throng of lawyers and witnesses. Again, Hale received her kindly. But this time Sir Henry Chester—who disliked Bunyan and had some ill-informed familiarity with his case—was standing near Hale. Interrupting Elizabeth, he told Hale that her husband had been duly convicted and that he was a hot-spirited fellow. He made other disparaging remarks. Hale seemed to give Chester's words some weight, for he said nothing more to Elizabeth. Tearfully, she turned away and was lost once more among the crowd that thronged the assize bench.[14]

It was then that Edmund Wylde, high sheriff of the Grove, Houghton Conquest, intervened. Seeing the disconsolate Elizabeth Bunyan make her way to the street outside, and having witnessed her unsuccessful petition to Hale, he approached her. In an act of great kindness, he told her there was yet another opportunity to see the judges before they left Bedford.

Elizabeth clutched at this hope like a lifeline and later made her way to "the Swan chamber, where the two judges and many justices and gentry of the county were in company together."

The scene that followed became one of the great chapters in the history of prisoners of conscience. She made her way forward amidst this circle of the great and powerful. Trembling, she turned to Hale and said, "My lord, I make bold to come once again to you." She then began to plead for her husband, asking Hale to take pity on him: "My lord," she said, "he is kept unlawfully in prison; they clapped him up before there was any proclamation against the meetings; the indictment also is false. Besides, they never asked him whether he was guilty or no; neither did he confess the indictment."[15]

At this, Judge Twisden spoke angrily to her. Sir Henry Chester was also severe, heartlessly repeating, "It is recorded, woman, it is recorded." Elizabeth summoned her courage. Turning to Hale, she told him how she had been to London—a serious journey for a peasant woman in those days—to see if she could obtain her husband's liberty. She said she had delivered a petition to Lord Barkwood, which he had shown to other peers in the House of Lords. They could not release him but had committed his releasement to the judges at the next assize. This was why she sought redress, she told Hale—she had come with a warrant from these peers.[16]

Hale seemed to not hear; but Chester persisted in saying, "He is convicted," and "It is recorded." Wishing to be rid of this troublesome woman, he told his colleagues that Bunyan "was a pestilent fellow, the like of whom there was not in the country."[17]

It was then that Judge Twisden interposed, asking, "Will your husband leave off preaching? If he will, you may send for him."

"My lord," she said, "he dares not [to stop] preaching as long as he can speak."

"Then there is nothing more to be done," Twisden said curtly. "He is a breaker of the peace."

"Not so, Lord," Elizabeth replied, "my husband desires to live peaceably, to follow his calling, and so maintain his family. There is a need for his release, my lord," she added, "for I have four small children that cannot help themselves, of which one is blind, and we have nothing to live upon but the charity of good people."[18]

"Hast thou four children?" Sir Matthew Hale asked. "Thou art but a young woman to have four children."

"My lord," Elizabeth said, "I am but mother-in-law to them, having not been married to him yet full two years. Indeed, I was with child when my husband was first apprehended; but being young and unaccustomed to such things, I was dismayed at the news, fell into labour, and so continued for eight days, and then was delivered; but my child died."

Deeply touched, Hale exclaimed, "Alas, poor woman!"

It was then that Twisden cruelly interrupted, saying, "Thou hast made poverty thy cloak. And, as I understand it, thy husband hath found it a much better thing to run up and down preaching than to follow his calling."

At this Hale asked, "What is his calling?" Several people from the assembled crowd spoke at once, saying, "A tinker, my lord!"

"Yes," Elizabeth acknowledged, "and because he is a tinker and a poor man, he is despised and cannot have justice."

Sir Henry Chester sensed Hale might be wavering. He had heard enough, and spoke to Hale with growing anger. "My lord, this man will preach and do whatever he wishes." It was as much as saying: "We cannot have this, nor can we permit it."

"No, my lord," Elizabeth said, "my husband preacheth nothing but the Word of God!"

Twisden, meanwhile, had become incensed at the temerity and presumption of this peasant woman—so much so that Elizabeth later told her husband she thought he was about to strike her.

"Preach the Word of God!" Twisden cried. "He runneth up and down and doeth harm."

"No, my lord," Elizabeth said, "it is not so; God hath owned him, and done much good by him."

"God!" exclaimed Twisden. "His doctrine is the doctrine of the devil!"

"My lord," Elizabeth said with a quiet, unyielding resolve, "when the righteous Judge shall appear, it will be known that my husband's doctrine is not the doctrine of the devil!"

Historians then and now have marveled at her courage and determination. "Elizabeth Bunyan was simply an English peasant woman," one of them wrote, "could she have spoken with more dignity had she been a crowned queen?"[19]

A sad denouement followed. All through that winter Bunyan remained in Bedford county gaol, and when, in 1662, the Spring Assizes came round again, he made a great effort to get his case brought on in court. But the justices and the clerk of the peace saw to it that although his name was at first inserted into the calendar of cases to be considered, it was later withdrawn. "Thus," Bunyan remembered, "was I hindered and prevented at that time also from appearing before the judge, and left in prison."[20]

Early in his imprisonment Bunyan suffered greatly. "When but a young prisoner," he wrote, it "lay much upon my spirit . . .

that my Imprisonment might end at the Gallows."[21] His greatest fear was not so much the way in which he would meet his end, but that he might not show the kind of courage that would give all to know that he died an undaunted Christian. "I thought [to] myself," he wrote, that "if I should make a scrabbling shift to clamber up the Ladder . . . I should either with quaking or other symptoms of faintings give occasion [for] reproach [of] the way of God and his People . . . This, therefore, lay with great trouble upon me, for methought I was ashamed to die with a pale Face and tottering Knees for such a cause as this."[22] In the midst of his anguish he cried out to God. And when he did, he seemed to find a courage not his own. It came to him that he might even upon the scaffold give the message of life to the crowd who came to see him die. "If it must be so," he thought, "if God will but convert one soul by my . . . last words, I shall not count my Life thrown away nor lost."[23] The threat of the gallows was never to be realized, but Bunyan had no way of knowing that. In the fearful present he knew, it was a very real prospect. He had need to make his peace. At his point of greatest need, he found that God was there to meet him. That thought would later infuse *The Pilgrim's Progress*.

≈

The county gaol in which Bunyan spent the next twelve years of his life was taken down in 1801.[24] It stood on the corner of the High Street and Silver Street—the latter so named because "it was the quarter where the Jews in early times trafficked in precious metals." Today a plaque in the pavement marks the spot where the gaol once stood.

John Brown wrote that "no sketch of the building . . . of any kind has come down to us." When Brown wrote his biography of Bunyan in the 1880s, he reported that "the only trace of the gaol still left was a rough stone wall . . . which was the wall of the small courtyard used by the prisoners."

However, a relic from the interior of the Bedford county gaol has survived: the prison door—a massive artifact made of "three transverse layers of oak, fastened through with iron bolts, [with] bars across an open centre." It is still preserved in the vestry of Bunyan Meeting Free Church in Bedford.

From John Brown we also learn that there were iron-grated windows on the Silver Street side of the county gaol. It was said that prisoners used to hang purses out of these windows on Sunday mornings, beseeching the help of such passers-by as were on their way to church or chapel. Beyond this, John Howard, the noted prison reformer of the 1700s, wrote that the gaol consisted mainly of a ground floor and second floor. The ground floor was for felons, and had two-day rooms, besides sleeping rooms. There were two dungeons underground, one situated in total darkness, and reached by a descent of eleven steps. The first floor, for debtors, consisted of four sleeping rooms and a common day room, also used for a chapel. All of the rooms were eight and a half feet high. There was also a small courtyard that was common to all the prisoners.[25]

Brown has provided an even more detailed description of Bunyan's place of confinement. He wrote:

The country gaol was probably not one of the worst in those times. It certainly was not so hideous as some . . . But very few prisons in England in the seventeenth century were even decent, and there is no reason to suppose that the one at Bedford was an exception to the general rule. Even in John Howard's time the day rooms were without fire-places, and the prisoners slept on straw, £5 a year being allowed to the gaoler for the purpose. In his day, too, gaol fever broke out, carrying off several of the prisoners, [as well as] William Daniel, the surgeon, and many of the townspeople outside.

Bunyan's prison possessions were few but precious. An account penned by a visitor whose name has not survived describes the possessions housed in his cell. "There," the visitor wrote, "I surveyed [Brother Bunyan's] library, the least and yet the best that ever I saw, consisting only of two books—a Bible and [Foxe's] 'Book of Martyrs.'"[26] Bunyan's copy of the latter was an edition dated 1641, in three volumes folio. At the foot of each of the three title pages he had written his name in large capital letters. These signatures were a statement of ownership, but they were also a testimony, as though he were saying, "I, too, know something of what it is to suffer."

Aside from this, the Bedford church doubtless provided Bunyan what aid they could—probably food and such items of clothing as they could spare. But, as John Brown wrote, "they could not do all they would. For many of them were themselves at various times his fellow-prisoners in Bedford gaol; others had to flee from their homes, to avoid arrest; and many were stripped of their possessions to pay the ruinous fines imposed upon them as Nonconformists."[27]

Because of his refusal to cease preaching, Bunyan could not

gain his release. But there were some mitigations of his confinement. Early on, he was granted a substantial measure of liberty over a period of six months between the Autumn Assizes of 1661 and the Spring Assizes of 1662. All the while, he did his utmost to get his name inserted in the calendar of prisoners for trial. Looking back on this, he wrote: "between these two assizes I had by my Jailor, some liberty granted me . . . I followed my wonted course of preaching, taking all occasions that was put into my hand to visit the people of God." On another occasion he wrote: "having somewhat more liberty I did go to see Christians at London."[28]

Such extraordinary liberty could not last. Bunyan's jailer had run a great risk, and soon enough the authorities who were so violently opposed to Bunyan got wind of what was going on. "My enemies," Bunyan wrote, "hearing of [the liberty granted to me] were so angry that they had almost cast my Jailor out of his place, threatening to indite him, and to do what they could against him . . . Whereupon my liberty was more straightened than it was before."[29]

Bunyan's hardships varied with the different officials who administered the gaol. From October 28, 1661, to October 9, 1668, a long period of seven years out of the twelve years of his imprisonment, his name does not occur once in the records of the Bedford church. For much of this time, John Brown reported, Bunyan was "under cruel and oppressive gaolers in an uncomfortable and close prison."[30]

He revealed something of what he felt during these years when he penned his *Prison Meditations* during the winter of 1662–63.[31] He crafted this work in response to a friend who had written to offer words of encouragement and solace. In reply, Bunyan said that while his gaolers might have imprisoned his body, his mind was still free.[32] He rendered his feelings in verse:

> ... though men keep my outward man
> Within their bolts and bars,
> Yet, by the faith of Christ, I can
> Mount higher than the stars.
> Here dwells good conscience, also peace,
> Here be my garments white;
> Here, though in bonds, I have release
> From guilt, which else would bite.
> The Truth and I, were both here cast
> Together, and we do
> Lie arm in arm, and so hold fast
> Each other: this is true.

At times, there was an easing of Bunyan's confinement. He was occasionally allowed short periods of parole, but it is not known precisely when they took place.[33] Perhaps the greatest concession he was granted was permission to work in order to support his family. He was not allowed to leave prison, but within its walls he was permitted to make "many hundred gross of long Tagg'd laces" for shoes, and so provide much-needed income for his family.

Aside from this, there seem to have been few or no prohibitions on visitors. Bunyan had a steady stream of them through the days and months and years. Still, one cannot lose sight of the toll that twelve years' imprisonment exacted. Bunyan was thirty-two when it began, and in the prime of life. He had a deep affection for his wife and children.

From the very beginning of Bunyan's confinement, he felt "like a man who at the bidding of conscience was pulling down his house upon the heads of those he loved best."[34] This was the cruelest part of the suffering he endured. Perhaps no other passage from his writings was written with greater feeling than this:

> The parting with my wife and poor children hath often been to me, in this place, as the pulling the flesh from the bones; and [I] have often brought to my mind the many hardships, miseries, and wants that my poor family was like to meet with . . . especially my poor blind child, who lay nearer my heart than all besides. Oh, the thoughts of the hardships I thought my poor blind one might go under, would break my heart to pieces!—Poor child! . . . What sorrow art thou like to have for thy portion in this world! Thou must . . . beg, suffer hunger, cold, nakedness, and a thousand calamities, [and] I cannot endure [that even] the wind should blow upon thee.[35]

No just account of all that Bunyan suffered in prison can be given. No brief mitigations of his confinement, however welcome, could compensate for the lost years and lost moments with his wife and family. He was a prisoner of conscience and suffered as such. A pardon for his release was issued on September 13, 1672. He was free, and there was an undeniable joy in that. But he and his family would also bear the scars of their ordeal for the rest of their lives.

"THE FORTUNATE LIMITS OF IMAGINATION"

I will instance, in our own language, *The Pilgrim's Progress* and *Robinson Crusoe*. Of all the prose works of fiction which we possess, these are, I will not say the best, but the most peculiar, the most unprecedented, the most inimitable. Had Bunyan and Defoe been educated gentlemen, they would probably have published translations and imitations of French romances "by a person of quality." I am not sure that we should have had Lear if Shakspeare had been able to read Sophocles.[1]

—Thomas Babington (Lord Macaulay)

I n the summer of 1658, Bunyan published one of his early works—a book with the truly ominous-sounding title of *A Few Sighs from Hell, or the Groans of a Damned Soul, &c., by that poor and contemptible servant of Jesus Christ, John*

Bunyan. This book, we learn from its title page, was printed in London "by Ralph Wood for M. Wright, at the King's Head in the Old Bailey."

Notwithstanding its title, *A Few Sighs from Hell* was from Bunyan's perspective a plea with the reader to embrace the gracious and merciful offers of salvation in Christ presented in Scripture. Bunyan felt he had escaped the fate described in the book's title. Finding grace and mercy, his book was intended as a cry from the heart.

He wished to rescue his readers from the fate he had so narrowly avoided. If his depictions of hellish torments were graphic (and they are), they were intended to underscore how precious a thing it was to be rescued—or, to put it in terms readers of Dante would understand, to be delivered from the torments of the inferno and receive the divine assurance of paradiso.

It seems incredulous that any kind of humor might be associated with a book bearing such a title, but there is. As it happened, Bunyan's book was published just a few days before Oliver Cromwell's death. As one would expect, the Lord Protector's demise was an occasion for public mourning (however much closet royalists must have rejoiced). And so the issue of the *Commonwealth Mercury* published for the week of September 2, 1658, came out with a deep black border, followed by the announcement of Cromwell's death. Immediately following this announcement came an advertisement: "There is lately published *A Few Sighs from Hell*, or the Groans of a Damned Soul, by John Bunyan." Centuries later, a discerning writer in *Notes and Queries* (Third Series, iii., 325) wondered whether the placement of this advertisement was a mere accident, or "a piece of malicious suggestion on the part of some royalist."[2]

But this was not the only instance of humor associated with Bunyan's book. Biographer John Brown, while acknowledging that "the drift of the book is serious," nonetheless identified "strokes of the writer's special humour" within its pages. There were rustic aphorisms of the kind Bunyan knew well, such as "the careless man lies like the smith's dog at the foot of the anvil, though the fire-sparks flee in his face." Other strokes of humor played satirically upon parables of Scripture, such as the story of the rich man and Lazarus found in the Gospel of Luke, chapter 16:

> Some men despise the Lazaruses of our Lord Jesus Christ because they are not gentlemen, because they cannot with Pontius Pilate speak Hebrew, Greek, and Latin. The rich man remembers how he slighted the Scriptures: "The Scriptures, thought I, what are they? A dead letter, a little ink and paper of three or four shillings price! Alas! what is the Scripture? Give me a ballad, a news-book, '*George on horseback*' or '*Bevis of Southampton*;' give me some book that teaches curious arts, that tells of old fables."[3]

Here, Bunyan ridiculed self-righteous religious hypocrites who made a show of great learning; or those who set such little store by Scripture and the care of their souls that they preferred the tales to be found in chapbooks to the consolations of holy writ.

But in this aside, Bunyan gave a rare glimpse of the kind of light reading with which he had been familiar all his life. And although he used these tales as a satirical reference point in *A Few Sighs from Hell*, he did not despise them. He was simply making a point about spiritual priorities in a way that his readers would readily understand.

Bunyan had never lost his relish for medieval romances like *Bevis of Southampton* or the legends surrounding St. George. They had fired his youthful imagination and fostered his great love of reading in the trying days after his formal education had ceased. They had provided him with many a happy hour when the day's work at the forge was done, and for this he had always remained grateful. He had lived within those books for a time, and his journeys in their pages had stayed with him.

This abiding interest in chivalric tales is shown with striking clarity in the plot of the First Part of *The Pilgrim's Progress*, written over an extended period during Bunyan's first imprisonment, probably from 1667 to 1672.[4] It was then that Bunyan remembered these tales. Once again, they were an imaginative refuge, and he wove elements of them into his matchless allegory. No less a commentator than C. S. Lewis spoke of this in one of his most celebrated lectures, "The Vision of John Bunyan." Lewis said:

> We may hazard a guess as to why [the inspiration for *The Pilgrim's Progress*] came at just that moment. My own guess is that the scheme of a journey with adventures suddenly reunited two things in Bunyan's mind which had hitherto lain far apart. One was his present and lifelong preoccupation with the spiritual life. The other, further away and longer ago, left behind (he had supposed) in childhood, was

his delight in old wives' tales and such last remnants of chivalric romance as he had found in chap-books. The one fitted the other like a glove. Now, as never before, the whole man was engaged.

The vehicle he had chosen—or, more accurately, the vehicle that had chosen him—involved a sort of descent. His high theme had to be brought down and incarnated on the level of an adventure story of the most unsophisticated type—a quest story, with lions, goblins, giants, dungeons and enchantments. But then there is a further descent. This adventure story itself is not left to the world of high romance. Whether by choice or by the fortunate limits of Bunyan's imagination—probably a bit of both—[*The Pilgrim's Progress* was] visualized in terms of the contemporary life that Bunyan knew.[5]

Several phrases in Lewis's lecture catch the reader's eye. "The fortunate limits of Bunyan's imagination" is among them. Lewis was, of course, referring to the relatively small number of books we can with certainty say that Bunyan read. Chief among these was the Authorized Version of the Bible; and historian J. R. Green echoed many a commentator down through the years when he observed: "so completely [did] the Bible become Bunyan's life that one feels its phrases as the natural expression of his thoughts. He . . . lived in the Bible till its words [had] become his own."[6]

But Lewis was equally just in drawing attention to Bunyan's "delight in old wives' tales and such last remnants of chivalric romance as he had found in chap-books." As a young man,

Bunyan had immersed himself in these writings. Now, with a power he found irresistible, the images, characters, and tropes of these tales seemed to give voice to "his present and life-long preoccupation with the spiritual life." For the first time he discerned their "secret affinity."[7] Seemingly disparate and distant experiences coalesced and were melded together. Now, this nascent and newly forged allegory began to clamor for his attention. C. S. Lewis has captured Bunyan's crowded hour of inspiration:

> To ask how a great book has come into existence is, I believe, often futile. But in this case Bunyan has told us the answer, so far as such things can be told. It comes in the very pedestrian verses prefixed to Part I [of *The Pilgrim's Progress*]. He says that while he was at work on quite a different book he "*Fell suddenly into an Allegory.*" He means, I take it, a little allegory, an extended metaphor that would have filled a single paragraph. He set down "*more than twenty things.*" And, this done, "*I twenty more had in my Crown.*" The "*things*" began "*to multiply*" like sparks flying out of a fire. They threatened, he says, to "*eat out*" the book he was working on. They insisted on splitting out from it and becoming a separate organism. He let them have their head. Then come the words which describe, better than any others I know, the golden hours of unimpeded composition:
>
> *For having now my Method by the end;*
> *Still as I pull'd, it came.*

It came. I doubt if we shall ever know more of the process called "inspiration" than those two monosyllables tell us.[8]

Somehow, separated from his family and confined within walls of thickset stone, John Bunyan discovered a grace that moved him to write. He heard a music that would not be bound by the door of his cell. Listening to it, he felt free and unfettered. He wrote as fast as the words and images came—and they came in quick profusion. There was a sureness about this story, he knew. It was in many ways his own. Time and again, as circumstances allowed, he returned to this burgeoning book during the last years of his first imprisonment—introducing new ideas and characters—faithfully fashioning his prose as the strokes of a brazier's hammer shape metal upon an anvil.

"FANCIES THAT LIT THE PRISON CELL"[1]

The First Part of *The Pilgrim's Progress*

The Pilgrim's Progress certainly exhibits all the marks of such a revival of primitive power and mystery . . . The description in Bunyan of how Moses came like a wind up the road, and was but a word and a blow; or how Apollyon straddled quite over the breadth of the way and swore by his infernal den—these are things which can only be paralleled in sudden and splendid phrases out of Homer or the Bible, such as the phrase about the monstrous and man-killing hands of Achilles, or the war-horse who laughs at the shaking of the spear.[2]

—G. K. Chesterton

As I walk'd through the wilderness of this world, I lighted on a certain place where was a Denn; And I laid me down in that place to sleep: And as I slept I dreamed a Dream."[3]

So begins *The Pilgrim's Progress*. Part knightly romance, part mystery play,[4] and in other ways wholly original—it was for the novelist George Eliot an example of "true genius manifested in [a] simple, vigorous, rhythmic style."[5] On the most basic level it was a quest story: recounting the journey of a pilgrim named Christian, amidst great trials, to find the Celestial City.

And it was written in prison. We know this because Bunyan himself has told us. In the third edition of *The Pilgrim's Progress*, published in 1679, there was an explanatory note in the margin alongside the word "Denn." It consisted of two words only, but those words settled beyond dispute the matter of where the book was written. The note read simply: "the gaol."[6]

The best scholarly research indicates that the bulk of the First Part of *The Pilgrim's Progress* appears to have been written during the final five years of Bunyan's first twelve-year imprisonment: perhaps beginning sometime in 1667 and ending around March 1772, when he was released.[7] He then knew the blessing of four years of freedom. Then he was imprisoned a second time—from December 11, 1676, to late June 1677. During this time, it is thought that Bunyan might well have made final revisions to the First Part—and perhaps wrote its Preface.[8]

But where, and when, was Bunyan imprisoned for a second time? The most reliable historical evidence indicates that in or about mid-December 1676 he was arrested by the sheriff of Bedfordshire.[9] Tradition holds that his incarceration, which lasted about six months (or until sometime before the end of June 1677), was in the gaol located on the Bedford town bridge.[10] And it was there, so the tradition runs, that Bunyan wrote much of the First Part of *The Pilgrim's Progress*.

Looking upon the antiquarian print of the Bedford town gaol in John Brown's Victorian biography, one is loath to part with this tradition. The print has the look of authenticity. The scene it depicts is one cherished by generations of readers and many biographers. It seems right that this was the place.

But it wasn't. In the years since Brown penned his biography, the bond has come to light for Bunyan's release in June 1677. And it reveals that his second imprisonment was in the Bedford county gaol.[11]

The circumstances of Bunyan's arrest in 1676 were these: He had neglected a summons to appear before the archdeacon's court in Bedfordshire, which, as a nonconformist, he was required by law to do. It was then that one of his old enemies, a Commissary of Bedford named William Foster, obtained a writ against him calling for his arrest under ancient laws regarding excommunication. Once Bunyan had been seized, several friends rallied to him. John Owen, the influential Puritan leader, appealed to Thomas Barlow, the Bishop of Lincoln (Owen's former tutor at Queen's College, Oxford) to secure Bunyan's release. Barlow was unwilling to do this on his own, fearing a hostile reprisal from his own enemies.[12] In a separate attempt, two members of another independent congregation expressed their willingness to enter into a bond for Bunyan's good behavior.[13] These early intercessions came to naught.

John Owen did Bunyan a good service. Although it took six or seven months, he kept trying to obtain Bunyan's release. Finally, through patient intercession with well-placed personal connections, and after posting what was called a "cautionary bond," Owen was able to obtain an order from Heneage Lord Finch directing the Bishop of Lincoln to release Bunyan.[14]

Prior to his release, Bunyan had not been idle. He was able to write and receive letters, which indicates his confinement was not particularly close or harsh.[15] Since friends and family could to all appearances visit him with some regularity, he could have been provided with the materials he needed to finish his revisions on the First Part of *The Pilgrim's Progress*. Seated at a rude table and chair, or perhaps only seated on a stool, he would have worked at his task.

Based upon the description of the Bedford county gaol given earlier, we know there were no provisions for a fire in Bunyan's cell against the winter cold of late December through January, February, and on into the spring of 1677. Once again, his saintly, long-suffering wife, Elizabeth, and their children were forced to shift for themselves—though in all likelihood members of Bunyan's congregation and sister churches provided some aid. His bed was likely one of straw, which would have served as a mattress and also as a partial covering against the cold. They were Spartan conditions at best.

In the summer days of June, when Bunyan emerged from his cell, the manuscript for the First Part of *The Pilgrim's Progress* had been completed. It was a book unlike any other he had written. Only the mysterious providence of his imprisonment had made it possible.

⁓

The Victorian biographer John Brown knew Bunyan's life and writings better than anyone in the nineteenth century. His summary of the First Part of *The Pilgrim's Progress* is as fine a synopsis as has been written. There is no better guide to take us through the essential elements of Bunyan's story.[16] And so we begin.

Walking through the wilderness of this world, the writer of *The Pilgrim's Progress* lights upon a den where he lays down to sleep. As he sleeps, he dreams, and sees a man clothed in rags, carrying a heavy burden and in deep anguish of soul.

Turning homeward, this man in rags, whose name is Christian, shares his distress with his wife and children, who conclude that some frenzy has seized him. They hope that a good night's sleep will settle him. But night brings no rest, the morning no relief; and with the day Christian wanders forth disconsolate.

In this condition he is met by Evangelist, who urges him to flee and tells him where he should go. He leaves at once as his counselor advises. Wife and children call after him in vain, and two of his neighbors bent on bringing him back by force are so far from succeeding, that one of them, Pliable by name, is prevailed upon to join him in his pilgrimage. These two, talking as they go of the glories of the heavens, are suddenly plunged into the miry Slough of Despond. Struggling out in rueful fashion, Pliable will have nothing more to do with these fine visions if this hazardous road is the one he must travel.

To Christian, however, the burden on his back is infinitely more grievous than any bedaubing of the Slough, and in the hope of getting rid of that, onward he goes. Turned out of his way by Mr. Worldly Wiseman, he is again set right by Evangelist, and reaches the wicket gate, where Good Will receives him.

Directed by this new friend, he reaches the house of Interpreter, where he sees things rare and profitable, pleasant and dreadful. On a wall there is the picture of a man who has eyes lifted up to heaven, the best of books in his hand, the law of truth upon his lips—a man who stood as if he pleaded with men. Besides this picture Christian sees also the symbols of Passion and Patience, of the fire not to be put out, of the man who in grim earnest fights his way into the palace. He sees images of a despairing soul in the iron cage, and of a man startled by dreams of judgment.

Leaving the House of Interpreter, Christian, to his joy, finds his weary burden fall off at the sight of the cross and is saluted by Shining Ones, who pronounce him forgiven. They clothe him with new raiment and set a mark upon his forehead. After this, he resumes his journey, passing by the characters of Simple, Sloth, Presumption, Formalist, and Hypocrite. He then climbs the Hill Difficulty to the arbor where he loses his roll, passes the lions, and reaches a stately palace, the name of which is Beautiful.

Here Christian is welcomed by a grave and beautiful damsel named Discretion, is entertained by Prudence, Piety, and Charity, and ultimately lodged in a large upper chamber named Peace, the window of which opened toward the sun rising, and where he sleeps till break of day. Here, as in the house of Interpreter, he sees many rarities, and in the armory is outfitted from head to foot and sent on his way.

After these pleasant experiences, Christian travels next to the Valley of Humiliation, where he is met by the fierce fiend Apollyon, a devil such as Luther met and Bunyan himself had known in his darkest moments of spiritual terror. Into this part of his allegory, he poured the most burning memories of his own life. The conflict that followed is the most stirring scene in the whole book,[17] and one of the greatest battle scenes in all literature:

> Then *Apollyon* strodled quite over the whole breadth of the way, and said . . . "Prepare thy self to dye; for I swear by my Infernal Den, that thou shalt go no farther: here will I spill thy soul . . ."
>
> Then did *Christian* draw, for he saw 'twas time to bestir him; and *Apollyon* as fast made at him, throwing Darts as thick as hail; by the which, notwithstanding all that *Christian* could do to avoid it, *Apollyon* wounded him in his *head*, his *hand*, and *foot*; this made *Christian* give a little back: *Apollyon* therefore followed his work amain, and *Christian* again took courage, and resisted as manfully as he could. This sore Combat lasted for above half a day . . .
>
> But as God would have it, while *Apollyon* was fetching his last blow, thereby to make a full end of this good Man, *Christian* nimbly reached out his hand for his Sword, and caught it, saying, *Rejoyce not against me, O mine enemy! when I fall, I shall arise;* and with that gave him a deadly thrust, which made him give back . . . and with that, *Apollyon* spread forth his Dragon's wings, and sped him away, that *Christian* saw him no more.[18]

Christian had no sooner escaped this terrible battle than he found himself among the fearsome shapes and doleful voices of

the Valley of the Shadow of Death.[19] It was a desolate place—
"a wilderness, a land of deserts and pits, a land of drought."
Here, Bunyan wrote:

> in the midst of this valley I perceived the mouth of hell to be,
> and it stood . . . hard by the wayside. Now, thought Christian,
> what shall I do? And ever and anon the flame and smoke would
> come out in such abundance, with sparks and hideous noises,
> (things that cared not for Christian's sword, as did Apollyon
> before) that he was forced to put up his sword, and betake
> himself to another weapon, called All-prayer, so he cried, in
> my hearing, O Lord, I beseech thee, deliver my soul.

Christian continued on for some time, disconsolate and
apprehensive. Then he heard the voice of a man who seemed to
be just ahead, saying, "Though I walk through the Valley of the
Shadow of Death, I will fear no evil, for thou art with me." He
went on; feeling here at least was some measure of hope. Before
long, the sun rose, and Christian was moved to say, "He hath
turned the shadow of death into the morning."

Christian then came upon Faithful, and in this good man
he found a kindred soul and traveling companion. They passed
through various dangers together—the caverns of the two
giants Pope and Pagan—they spoke of past experiences—and
they eluded the snares of deception laid for them by "Talkative,
the son of Say-well, of Prating Row, a man of facile tongue and
slippery life."

Upon Talkative's departure, they were joined by Evangelist.
But their joy at seeing him was tempered by dire words of

prophecy: one of them would not survive their encounter with the people of Vanity Fair. "When you are come to the Town," Evangelist said, you "shall find fulfilled what I have [said] . . . quit yourselves like men; and commit the keeping of your souls to your God."[20]

The conception for Vanity Fair, wrote John Brown, "was doubtless suggested to Bunyan by one of the many fairs held in his days. Elstow Fair had been a great institution ever since Henry II had granted a charter to the nuns of the Abbey there." But, Brown continued:

> the one fair of all others likely to suggest and be the historical basis of Vanity Fair, was that held for centuries at Sturbridge, near to Cambridge. . . . It was a vast emporium of commerce. Mercers from France brought their silks, and Flemings from the Low Countries their woollens; traders from Scotland and from Kendal set forth their pack-horses on the road to be in time for the fair, while barges from London came round by Lynn and brought the merchandise of the city along the Ouse and the Cam. All new discoveries and foreign acquisitions were here first brought to public view. . . . Bunyan, often in the neighbourhood of Cambridge, as we know he was, must several times in his life have looked on this remarkable scene at Sturbridge, a scene which lent itself so readily to the purposes of his allegory.[21]

As conceived by Bunyan, Vanity Fair was a den of iniquity, replete with jugglers, cheats, games, plays, fools, exotic creatures, and knaves of every kind. It had its "great one of the fair," its court of justice, and its power of judgment. True to Evangelist's prophecy, Christian and Faithful were seized by the authorities. Faithful was sentenced to death after a farce of a trial. He was burnt at the stake and received a martyr's crown. Christian barely escaped with his life. Mourning his friend, he had to go on alone.

But not so very far, for Christian soon came upon a man named Hopeful, who became Faithful's successor in the pilgrimage.

The sorrows of Vanity Fair were scarcely behind them when they encountered a man named By-ends—"a subtle evasive knave" who tried to lure Christian and Hopeful from the road to the Celestial City. They resisted his fair-seeming words and the temptations he proffered.

By-ends had no sooner left than they came upon Demas and his silver mine. He offered riches, which they refused. Leaving him, they came upon a strange sight: a pillar of salt in the shape of a woman. It bore a sobering inscription: "Remember Lot's Wife." Reminded here how easily one can come to ruin, they pressed on. Soon, they found themselves along the banks of "a pleasant river lined with fruitful trees." Here they rested and were refreshed.

Resuming their journey, they came within sight of "the grim walls of Doubting Castle." Here they were captured by the Giant Despair, but eventually gained their release through the use of a key of Promise. Having made good their escape, they soon came to the foothills of the Delectable Mountains, where they were met by kindly Shepherds.

Strengthened anew, Christian and Hopeful set upon the

road once more. New opponents awaited them, Flatterer and Atheist, but they passed through this dangerous region safely and entered the Country of Beulah—a land of flowers and singing birds "where the air is very sweet and pleasant and the sun shineth night and day—a land where the angels come, for it is on the borders of heaven."

One trial yet remained: the crossing of a bridgeless river—a river which men found deeper or shallower as their belief in the King of the Celestial City waxed strong or wavered. At the last, Hopeful proved the truest of friends—helping Christian gain the far shore. Once there, they were joyfully received and taken to the city beyond. Bells rang out in welcome as they entered its gates.

"BUNYAN'S IMMORTAL STORY"[1]

The Second Part of *The Pilgrim's Progress*

The fictional character [Theodore] Roosevelt most admired was Greatheart, Christiana's guide in [the Second Part of] Bunyan's *Pilgrim's Progress*. [As president, Roosevelt] frequently alluded to this literary hero to underscore his arguments. "We gird up our loins as a nation . . . to play our part manfully in winning the ultimate triumph . . . and with unfaltering steps tread the rough road of endeavor . . . battling for the right, as Greatheart . . . battled."[2]

—G. S. Smith

The Second Part of *The Pilgrim's Progress* is as beloved a story as there is in Western literature, and we owe its composition (at least in part) to a fraud, an unexpected rivalry, and a failed first attempt by Bunyan to craft a sequel.

Bunyan had intended *The Life and Death of Mr. Badman*

(published in 1680) to be a sequel to *The Pilgrim's Progress*. He had not expected the striking success *The Pilgrim's Progress* had met with (going through three editions in a year).[3] And so it was inevitable that he should contemplate a sequel. He had, indeed, hinted at this at the close of the First Part, saying that if his reader were "Cast away all as vain/I know not but 'twill make me dream again."[4]

But how to do it? It seemed a good idea "to complete the picture [begun in the First Part] by a contrast." Bunyan, as John Brown observed, had "given the story of a noble life . . . a life whose course was upward to the City of God; his purpose now was to paint in shadow the story of a life steering for the outer darkness, of a soul ever 'unmaking itself.'"[5]

When the third edition of *The Pilgrim's Progress* was published in 1679, Bunyan began to work in earnest on *The Life and Death of Mr. Badman*. He wrote quickly and in a burst of creativity. The resulting manuscript was published in 1680.

In Bunyan's mind, there was a close connection between the two books. As he stated in the Preface to *Badman*:

> As I was considering with myself what I had written concerning the Progress of the Pilgrim from this world to glory: and how it had been acceptable to many in this nation: It came again into my mind to write, as then of him that was going to Heaven, so now of the Life and Death of the Ungodly and of their travel from this world to Hell.[6]

But, Brown wrote, "whatever Bunyan's intention might be, the popular instinct was in this case truer than his own." The public wanted to revisit the world of *The Pilgrim's Progress*, not a world that marked the descent of a soul that was damned.

Not that *Badman* was a substandard book. Far from it. It has been hailed by subsequent critics as a precursor to the modern novel and was thus an important artistic achievement. But ultimately, so far as Bunyan's newfound audience was concerned, "the story of Badman's Life only served as a foil to that of Christian; and could not be accepted either as its complement or continuation."[7]

This was made painfully clear to Bunyan when other writers, who cheerfully ignored *Badman*, took it upon themselves to complete *The Pilgrim's Progress* for him. In 1683 a writer who published under the initials T. S. stepped forward. His book bore the title: *The Second Part of the Pilgrim's Progress, from this present World of Wickedness and Misery to An Eternity of Holiness and Felicity: Exactly Described under the Similitude of a Dream.* T. S.'s canny publisher made sure the book closely resembled Bunyan's work both in terms of its size and typeface.[8]

Still, T. S. was not devious, even if his book was a turgid rehash bent on doctrinal correctness and less fanciful imaginative wanderings. Not surprisingly, it disappeared with scarcely a ripple.

But this was not the unkindest cut. When Bunyan published the genuine Second Part to *The Pilgrim's Progress* in early 1685, he told his readers (in verse) what many of them already knew: *several* fraudulent "Second Parts" had been previously published.

> Some have of late to counterfeit
> My Pilgrim, to their own my title set;

> Yea others, half my name and title too
> Have stitched to their own book to make them do
> But yet they by their Features do declare
> Themselves not mine to be whose'er they are.[9]

Taken together, the circumstances that led Bunyan to make a second attempt at a sequel to the First Part of *The Pilgrim's Progress* were strange. But in the end, the only way to thwart counterfeiters who wished to capitalize on the first book's success was to write another.

Notwithstanding this, Bunyan was too gifted an artist to craft a poorly conceived sequel. Indeed, there is every reason to believe that once he had taken up his pen, he found renewed inspiration. For a start, he was not imprisoned when he wrote the Second Part. And it is hard not to think that its more pastoral style owes much to his reunion with his family. The First Part was written amidst great adversity; the Second Part in better times. Writing with his family gathered about him was an unlooked-for blessing.

To be sure, there are similarities between the First and Second Parts. If Bunyan's readers wished to revisit the world evoked in the First Part, he would accommodate them. What is more, there were new elements that his restlessly fertile mind could introduce. He relished the prospect.

Unlike writing the First Part, Bunyan as the writer is no longer in his den—that is, he was no longer in prison.[10] Straightaway, readers find him in the more pleasant pastoral setting of a woodland lodge. It is there, in a place of peace, that his second vision unfolds.

Bunyan next introduced a narrative device he had never used before: a character who relates the prologue of the story. This, we learn from John Brown, was "an expedient similar to the device of Euripides among the Greek tragedians, who introduces some hero or god in the prologue of the story to tell us what is the present state of affairs, and what has happened up to the time of his speaking."

Bunyan called this aged interpreter Mr. Sagacity. Bunyan, in the guise of a dreamer (as in the First Part), is approached by Mr. Sagacity, who describes how Christiana (the wife of Christian) was led to go forth on pilgrimage. Mr. Sagacity carries the narrative forward as far as the familiar scene at the wicket-gate, whereupon he leaves—to be seen no more.

As with Christian, Christiana's setting forth makes a stir among the neighbors. And while Obstinate and Pliable had tried to turn Christian from his purpose, Mrs. Timorous and Neighbour Mercy come on the same errand to Christiana.

In the First Part, after talking with Christian, Pliable had decided to go on with him. So, too, Neighbour Mercy decides to go on with Christiana. However, in the First Part Pliable had turned back when faced with adversity; Mercy does not.

John Brown wrote:

The second part of *The Pilgrim's Progress* lies along the same main lines as the first. We have the City of Destruction, the Wicket-gate, the House of Interpreter, the Hill Difficulty, the Palace Beautiful, the Valley of Humiliation and that of the Shadow of Death, Vanity Fair, the Delectable Mountains, the Enchanted Ground, the Land of Beulah, and the River without a bridge. We meet with some of the same people along the road or some of their relations, and all through the journey the pilgrims find that every one knows Christiana's husband, and the mere mention of his name proves a passport to hospitality and honour for her and her children.[11]

The Second Part of Bunyan's allegory was in many ways a reunion with characters and scenes readers had taken to heart. The scenes of domestic happiness depicted in it were a mirror of the domestic happiness Bunyan knew in the early 1680s. Out of prison, and reunited with his family, he had been granted a measure of personal peace and happiness unlike any he had yet experienced.

Still there were new elements and variations to be found. Once more, John Brown wrote about what these were:

> In the House of Interpreter the later pilgrims see in the significant rooms sights which Christian saw not. They are shown the man who could look no way but downward, and who went on raking sticks and straws and dust of the floor, all unmindful of the celestial crown to be seen over his head; the spider which, repellent creature as it is, yet finds its way into kings' palaces . . .
>
> In the Palace Beautiful . . . they were shown additional rarities: one of the apples that Eve did eat of; Jacob's ladder, on which the angels were going up and coming down; the mount on which Abraham offered up his son Isaac.

In all of these scenes, Bunyan revealed a many-sided sympathy for the variety to be found in spiritual experience.[12] This can be seen as well in the contrasts between the First and Second Parts:

> Few things are more marked in the story than the contrast between the Valley of Humiliation as it presented itself to Christian, and as it presented itself to those who came after him—to the man of high spirit and to the women queenly in their passive meekness. To him it was a scene of awful conflict with Apollyon, to them it was a tranquil dwelling in green pastures and by still waters. To the sweet, contented spirit of Mercy this valley was a place where she loved to be . . .

The gentle nature of Mr. Fearing, too, found in this valley [a] congenial home. "Here he would lie down, embrace the ground, and kiss the very flowers that grew in this valley. He would now be up every morning by break of day, tracing and walking to and fro in this valley."[13] It is a valley that to the meek and lowly in heart is ever green.

≈

If a poll were to be taken, the favorite character encountered by Christiana and her family might well be that of Greatheart. Knight-errant, slayer of the Giant-Grim, and ever-faithful friend, Greatheart was the embodiment of chivalric romance cast in Christian mythos. Few fictional characters were as familiar to Victorians in Britain and America as he. From the family of Theodore Roosevelt to the humblest cottage in Britain, he was known and loved.

Still, as John Brown observed, "none of Bunyan's creations ever laid deeper hold of his heart than did Mr. Fearing, who was dejected at every difficulty, and stumbled at every straw." Bunyan never forgot that the early years of his pilgrimage were a time when he walked with halting steps and slow. Many might wish to be a Greatheart; but Bunyan had words of comfort for those who, like him, had been at times like Mr. Fearing.

Bunyan's ready sympathy for those who struggled was written into other characters—Mr. Feeblemind, Mr. Ready-to-halt, Mr. Despondency, and his daughter, Miss Much-afraid. The way of grace was revealed to them in the persons of Mercy and Christiana, and it is hard not to think that here Bunyan remembered and paid tribute to the women in his own life who had pointed him to the way of grace—his mother, his first wife, the three or four women who talked of the things of God in the sun, and his second wife, Elizabeth, who had taken up the cause of his imprisonment before the great and powerful. In ways that he knew well, they had been his champions.

Then there were passages in the Second Part of *The Pilgrim's Progress* so well known on a time as to be proverbial. One thinks here of the Monument to Christian's Victory over Apollyon, and the lines inscribed upon it:

> Hard by here was a Battle fought,
> Most strange, and yet most true;
> Christian and Apollyon sought
> Each other to subdue.
> The Man so bravely play'd the Man,
> He made the Fiend to fly;

Of which a Monument I stand,
The same to testify.

John Brown's summary of the Second Part of *The Pilgrim's Progress* is apposite and just. "It carries with it," he wrote, "sufficient impress of Bunyan's genius, enough of charm and individuality all its own to entitle Christiana to go hand-in-hand with Christian on his pilgrimage through time. Between these two there is a vital relation: they are the creations of the same genial soul."[14]

The Second Part of *The Pilgrim's Progress* was a complementary flowering of the artistic gifts Bunyan displayed in the First Part. If the First Part described a pilgrimage marked by danger, hardship, suffering, and final victory, the Second Part delved more deeply into the moments of joy and charity, sympathy and solace that also unfold amidst a pilgrimage. Moments of high courage and martial prowess were undoubtedly present, but there were new elements and a richness of experience to be found as well.

"GREAT EXTREMES"[1]

> During these politically stirring times, Bunyan went
> on writing his books . . . looking out upon the storm,
> not knowing whether it would blow him to the haven
> of settled liberty or once more on to the rocks of
> prison.[2]
>
> —John Brown

In the last ten years of his life, John Bunyan became a great
public figure. People took to calling him "Bishop Bunyan"
and flocked to hear him preach. One sermon he delivered
at a meetinghouse in London drew a thousand people to hear him
at seven in the morning. Readers in the New England colonies
knew *The Pilgrim's Progress* almost as well as readers in England
itself.[3] Bunyan's influence spread to continental Europe. Within
his lifetime, *The Pilgrim's Progress* was translated into Welsh,
French, and Dutch.[4]

Nothing underscores the stature Bunyan had attained better than a story involving the learned Puritan divine John Owen and King Charles II. As recounted by the poet Robert Southey, the king asked Owen "how a learned man such as he could sit and listen to an illiterate tinker." Owen replied, "May it please your Majesty, could I possess that tinker's abilities for preaching, I would most gladly relinquish all my learning."[5]

But there is something of a cautionary tale in the last decade of Bunyan's life. True, it was in many ways his most important decade as an author. The distinguished biographer Roger Sharrock reported that Bunyan's fame during these years "gave him the confidence to continue his exploration of the imaginatively freer forms of the religious allegory and the improving novel. *The Life and Death of Mr. Badman* came in 1680 . . . followed by *The Holy War* in 1682, and the Second Part of *The Pilgrim's Progress* in 1684. All this time the flow of published sermons did not diminish."[6]

Still the shadow of war or persecution was never very far away. When James II ascended the throne in February 1685, it precipitated the violently suppressed Monmouth Rebellion and a last great wave of persecution for dissenters.[7]

Amidst such pervasive violence and uncertainty, Bunyan feared imprisonment for a third time. In a deed of gift drawn up in December 1685, he transferred all his property to his "well-beloved wife, Elizabeth Bunyan." The reason for this unusual step, John Brown wrote, "[was] obvious enough. In the then state of public feeling he might any day be 'had home to prison' again, his property confiscated, and his family thrown homeless upon the world. To protect them even if he should be deprived of his liberty, he made over everything in legal form to his wife."[8]

But the unpredictable policies of James were not yet done with Bunyan. In 1687, just one year before his death, the king sought to conciliate dissenters—that he might thereby generate popular support for the toleration of Catholics. Incredibly, an olive branch was extended from James to Bunyan through Lord Aylesbury. The offer of a government post was held out, but Bunyan refused.[9] Instead, he was content to lend whatever prestige he had to obtain seats for members of his church on the reorganized corporation of Bedford. He had seen enough of kings, war, and persecution. He had no wish to dabble in high politics, and it says something for his character that James's offer held no fascination for him. He was a brazier's son. He would leave the world a brazier's son. It was enough to do what he could to secure the future of his church through shoring up its support among officials in local government.

In his final years, Bunyan had gained a hard-won wisdom. The comings and goings of kings, civil wars, persecutions, and imprisonments—he had seen and known all of these. They seem to have been much in his thoughts when he published an enigmatic work called *Seasonable Counsel; or, Advice to Sufferers.* In its Introduction, he spoke of "times that try us [and] make us to know ourselves"—and "days that bend and humble us." Do we not see, he asked, how such days redound to our ultimate benefit? "We could not live . . . if we had not our seasonable winters." He closed with something like a benediction: "The Lord bless all seasons to his people, and help them rightly to [acquit] themselves, under all the times that go over them."[10]

Religious conflict had ravaged England for as long as Bunyan could remember. All this time, men had seemed bent on exorcising the better angels of their nature.

Now, near the end of his life, he wished nothing more than "to show my loyalty to the king . . . my love to my fellow-subjects and my desire that all Christians should walk in ways of peace and truth."[11]

THE HOUSE ON
SNOW HILL

[Bunyan's] end was characteristic. It was brought on
by exposure [to harsh weather] when he was engaged
in an act of charity.[1]

—James Anthony Froude

In mid-August 1688, fifty-nine-year-old John Bunyan traveled to the town of Reading. His purpose was to preach; but he had another errand as well. A young neighbor had approached him with a troubling story. The young man had, he said, deeply offended his father—so much so that there seemed no hope of reconciliation. He now faced the very real threat of being disinherited.[2]

Bunyan's heart went out to his neighbor. Perhaps he saw a bit of his younger self standing before him—a brash, impulsive young man who needed taking in hand, as he once had.

Whatever his thoughts may have been, Bunyan agreed to intercede. He sought an interview with the young man's father and they talked for a long while. Bunyan spoke of the evils of anger and passion, and may well have shared how these had gotten the better of him in his younger days. He had in after years been better taught. Long experience had proved the value of love and reconciliation many times over. "Can you not," he asked his host, "forgive your son?"

Moved by this entreaty, the father agreed, and Bunyan left the interview knowing he had done a good service. He mounted his horse and continued on to London, where he had also planned to preach. At some point on the road, he saw storm clouds gather. A few moments more and a chilling rain began, thoroughly drenching him. He rode on for many dreary miles before reaching the home of his friend, John Strudwick, a grocer and chandler at the sign of the Star, on Snow Hill, near Holborn Bridge.[3] As Bunyan reined in his horse, the thirty-four-year-old Strudwick emerged from the storefront door. It was a terrible time to be on the road, and Brother Bunyan was not a young man.

Strudwick had reason to be concerned. A flu epidemic had recently been reported in a newsletter. Still another observer described its symptoms: "it seizes like a giddiness of the head and . . . ague [runs] throwout the whole body. They say three parts of the City have had it."[4]

Bunyan gratefully entered Strudwick's house and changed his wet clothes. He was doubtless taken to sit by a fire and provided with food, perhaps a stew, that would help to warm him. As he felt the warmth of the fire, his thoughts may have turned to the sermons he soon had to give in the city. Before long, he would have gone to his room, grateful for rest and a good bed.

The Sunday sermon Bunyan delivered at Whitechapel on August 19 was a memorable one. He spoke of escape from "the Dark Dungeon of Sin," and the glory of Christ's resurrection from the grave. He described how the righteousness of God enveloped those who had come to faith.[5] It was his story, he said to those who heard him. It could be theirs.

It is possible that even as he was speaking, Bunyan knew he was not well. Returning to Strudwick's home, he soon became gravely ill. He may have contracted influenza, but it was just as likely he had been stricken with pneumonia. He had few physical reserves to draw upon. Some years before, he had narrowly escaped a sickness thought to be consumption. He had also suffered physically during the many years of his imprisonment.[6]

Soon a "violent fever" and "sweating distemper" racked his body. For ten days he lingered, even as every effort was made to save his life. It is not known for certain if word ever reached his wife, Elizabeth, and their children in time for them to be by his side. As it was, such news would have taken several days to reach them, and several days more for them to reach him.[7]

Throughout his ordeal, Bunyan was attended by such friends as were close at hand. One of them, George Cokayn, always remembered what he saw. He described the way Brother Bunyan bore himself while dying:

> with much constancy and patience; and expressed himself to us if he desired nothing more than to be dissolved and to be with Christ . . .
>
> [F]inding his vital strength decay [and] having settled his

mind and affairs as well as the shortness of his time and the violence of his disease would admit . . . he resigned his soul into the hands of his most merciful Redeemer.[8]

On Friday, August 31, 1688, John Bunyan died in a house that was not his own. But then, for so many years, he had been a pilgrim. Now he had passed over. All struggles and conflict had ceased. He would know, at last, a peace without end.

EPILOGUE

Relics

Oh, then come hither, And lay my book, thy head,
and heart together.

—John Bunyan

Midway between Oxford and Cambridge lies the town of Bedford. There, on Mill Street, is the John Bunyan Museum. Among its many treasured possessions are several relics he once owned. Two were made by him: a wooden flute and a metal violin that is a testament to his great skill as a metalsmith.

There are legends associated with both. The first concerns the flute, said to have been made from the leg of a three-legged stool that belonged to Bunyan during one of his imprisonments. When he was unobserved, so the story goes, he would remove the flute from its place in the stool and play it. Should one of the guards come toward his cell upon hearing its music, Bunyan would quickly replace the flute in its hole and sit on the stool, thus concealing it. The flute can be seen to this day, and it is pleasant to think the legend true in all particulars. Bunyan had been imprisoned for preaching the gospel, but he still found a way to be heard—albeit in simple melodies played upon a hand-carved flute. He would not be silent.

It is not known precisely when Bunyan made his metal violin, but it, too, has a story. It was made from sheet iron and attests his best skill as an artisan. Why did he make it? We cannot be sure, but it is difficult not to think he did because it was a true test of his craft.

One can almost hear a neighbor saying, "Friend John, violins are made of wood. Best to let a luthier try his skill; the making of such things lies beyond you." Bunyan did not back away from challenges, and he would have warmed to this one. "I will make the trial," he might well have said.

The resulting instrument is graceful—finely shaped and seamless. Charcoal grey in color, it looks as though it may have been cast in metal rather than fashioned from welded sheet iron. Those who have played it say that it has a remarkably fine tone.[1] Bunyan was no Stradivarius, it is true, but his finely crafted violin endures—ready to make music if called upon.

And that is so like John Bunyan himself. Writing books in prison is never easily done, even under the best circumstances, and he had known many kinds of suffering. It is an achievement on another order of magnitude entirely to have crafted a masterpiece in such a setting, as he did. For one focused moment in time, he was able to summon all of his skill as an artist—all of his life experiences—and pour them into one book, even as he might have poured molten, refined metal into a mold and found the result to be one peerless example of the brazier's art. *The Pilgrim's Progress* is a matchless alloy of imagery, plot, and language "written cleane and pure."[2] Three hundred and thirty

years after its publication, the influence of this improbable masterwork is not yet spent. It still endures; and will endure, so
long as people are drawn to the music of the written word and
the triumph of the human spirit.

APPENDIX:
A BUNYAN TIMELINE

1603–25 James I reigns as king of England.

1608 John Milton is born on December 9.

1615 Theologian and divine Richard Baxter is born on November 12.

1616 William Shakespeare dies on April 23.

1618–48 Thirty Years War begins as a conflict between Protestants and Catholics within the Holy Roman Empire. Over time, nearly all of continental Europe becomes involved.

1620 Landing of Pilgrims in America aboard the *Mayflower*.

1623 Blaise Pascal is born on June 19.

1625–49 Charles I reigns as king of England.

1628 John Bunyan is born. The date of his birth is unknown, but he was baptized on November 30. He is the eldest of three children born to Thomas Bunyan (1603–76) and Margaret (Bentley) Bunyan (1603–44).

1636 Harvard College is founded in America.

1642–45 Civil war in England between parliamentary and royalist armies.

1643 Sir Isaac Newton is born on January 4.

1644 Bunyan's mother dies. Several months later, he becomes a soldier in the parliamentary army.

1645 In June, the parliamentary army is victorious at the battle of Naseby.

1647 In July, Bunyan is demobilized from the army.

1648–49 Second civil war in England between parliamentary and royalist armies.

1649 Bunyan marries his first wife (whose name is unknown). The trial and execution of Charles I takes place.

1650–58 Period during which Bunyan's slow spiritual transformation takes place (according to biographer Richard Greaves).

1650 Bunyan's blind daughter Mary is born (she is baptized on July 30). Richard Baxter publishes *The Saint's Everlasting Rest*.

1653–58 Protectorate of Oliver Cromwell.

1655 Bunyan is sent out as a preacher by the leaders of his church in Bedford.

1658 Bunyan's first wife dies. Death of Oliver Cromwell on September 3.

1659 Richard Cromwell abdicates, after briefly succeeding his father.

1660 Restoration of Stuart monarchy under Charles II. Bunyan is arrested in November. His second and newly wedded wife Elizabeth miscarries.

1660–72 The time of Bunyan's first imprisonment in the Bedford county gaol.

1662 Pascal dies on August 19.

1665 Bunyan publishes *The Holy City*. The Great Plague engulfs London. It kills between 75,000 and 100,000 of London's rapidly expanding population of about 460,000.

1666 Bunyan publishes his spiritual autobiography *Grace Abounding*. The Great Fire of London consumes much of the city. In Lincolnshire, Isaac Newton sees an apple fall from a tree at his mother's home and begins to formulate his theories about gravity.

1667 Milton's *Paradise Lost* is published.

1667–72 The period, according to Roger Sharrock, in which Bunyan probably wrote the First Part of *The Pilgrim's Progress*.

1668 According to the magisterial biography written by Richard Greaves, Bunyan begins work on *The Pilgrim's Progress*, the First Part, in or about March of this year.

1670 Pascal's *Pensees* is published posthumously.

1672 After twelve years, Bunyan is released from prison in March.

1674 Milton dies on November 8.

1676–77 Bunyan is imprisoned for a second time (from December 1676 to June 1677).

1678   Bunyan publishes the First Part of *The Pilgrim's Progress*.

1680   Bunyan publishes *The Life and Death of Mr. Badman*.

1681   The first American edition of *The Pilgrim's Progress* is published by Samuel Green of Boston.

1682   Bunyan publishes *The Holy War*.

1684   Bunyan publishes the Second Part of *The Pilgrim's Progress*.

1685   Death of Charles II. James II becomes king. In what would come to be known as the "Bloody Azzizes," Judge George Jeffreys sentences thousands to death or transportation into slavery in the wake of the failed Monmouth Rebellion.
Bunyan fears a third imprisonment and hides a Deed of Gift in the chimney of his cottage so that his property will not be seized. It lies hidden there until its discovery in 1838.
Richard Baxter, aged seventy, is imprisoned, and remains so for eighteen months.

1687   Isaac Newton's *Principia Mathematica* is published.

1688   Bunyan dies on August 31. In November, William of Orange lands in England at the head of a twenty-thousand-man army. Soon after, the deposed king, James II, escapes and leaves England, never to return. In America, Pennsylvanian Mennonites issue a first formal protest against slavery.

1689   William and Mary are crowned king and queen.

1691   Richard Baxter dies on December 8.

NOTES

PREFACE

1. *A Complete Manual of English Literature* (New York: Sheldon & Company, 1871), 221.
2. G. K. Chesterton, *George Bernard Shaw* (New York: John Lane Company, 1909), 101–02.
3. George Barrell Cheever, *Lectures on The Pilgrim's Progress* (London: A Fullarton and Co., 1846), 1.

PROLOGUE

1. Simon Winchester, *The Meaning of Everything* (New York, HarperCollins, 2003), xvii, xxi.
2. "Examining the OED," an article posted on the Web site: http://oed.hertford.ox.ac.uk/main/content/view/139/306/.
3. J. W. Cross, ed., *George Eliot's Life, as Related in Her Letters and Journals*, vol. 2 (Boston: Estes and Lauriat, 1895), 110.
4. See Sue Le Blond's article "Sunday in the East Room: Mansfield Park, Chapters 18 and 32," posted on the Web site: http://www.janeausten.co.uk/magazine/page.ihtml?pid=231&step=4.
5. See Andrew Wright's review of *Only a Novel: The Double Life of Jane Austen* by Jane Aiken Hodge, in JSTOR, Vol. 27, No. 4 (March 1973), 495–97.
6. See *The Cambridge Companion to Harriet Beecher Stowe* for the significant references to Bunyan in Stowe's works. See also the article "Religion in Uncle Tom's Cabin," from the Web site: http://xroads.virginia.edu/~ma02/harris/utc/lesson6.html.
7. A citation from Part 5 of Stowe's *Sunny Memories of Foreign Lands* (1854).
8. See Pat Rogers's essay on Johnson in *The New Oxford Dictionary of National Biography*.
9. From Chapter 28 of James Boswell's *Life of Samuel Johnson*.
10. The Letters of Robert Louis Stevenson, vol. 1, chapter 6
11. Graham Balfour, *The Life of Robert Louis Stevenson* (London: Methuen and Co., 1906), 33.
12. As stated on pages 116–17 of Graham Balfour, *The Life of Robert Louis Stevenson*, vol. 1 (New York: Charles Scribner's Sons, 1901). See also Stevenson's essay "Books Which Have Influenced Me," in his *Later Essays*.

13. John Bunyan, *The Pilgrim's Progress*, Introduction by R. L. Stevenson, 7th ed. (London: Samuel Bagster and Sons, Ltd., 1909).

14. Salter, Mary Jo, "Louisa May Alcott's American Girls," published in the *New York Times* on May 15, 2005.

15. Robert Stanton, "Hawthorne, Bunyan, and the American Romances," *PMLA*, Vol. 71, No. 1 (March 1956), 155–65.

16. See *Hawthorne*, by Henry James III, Early Writings.

17. George Parsons Lathrop, *A Study of Hawthorne* (Boston, 1886), 30–37, 69–73; F. O. Matthiesson, *American Renaissance* (New York, 1941), 195–99, 273; W. Stacy Johnson, "Hawthorne and *The Pilgrim's Progress*," *JEGP*, I, (1951), 166.

18. Robert Stanton, "Hawthorne, Bunyan, and the American Romances," *PMLA*, Vol. 71, No. 1 (March 1956), 155–65. Stanton identifies the echoes of Bunyan, whilst the allusions to Bunyan in Hawthorne's writings are identified in the following sources: George Parsons Lathrop, *A Study of Hawthorne* (Boston, 1886), 30–37, 69–73; F. O. Matthiesson, *American Renaissance* (New York, 1941), 195–99, 273; W. Stacy Johnson, "Hawthorne and *The Pilgrim's Progress*," *JEGP*, I (1951), 166.

19. More explicitly still, Twain titled his bestselling 1869 book *Innocents Abroad, or The New Pilgrim's Progress*. It was the biggest bestseller Twain had during his lifetime.

20. Albert Bigelow Paine, *Mark Twain: A Biography*, vol. 2 (New York: Harper and Brothers, 1912), 871–72.

21. In the December 23, 1908, issue of the *New York Times*, a letter from Theodore Roosevelt is quoted in which he writes: "Great Heart is my favorite character in allegory . . . just as Bunyan's 'Pilgrim's Progress' is to my mind one of the greatest books that ever was written; and I think Abraham Lincoln is the ideal Great Heart of public life."

22. Information gleaned from the following Web site: http://hcl.harvard.edu/libraries/houghton/collections/past_exhibits.html.

23. Ibid.

24. See J. Karl Franson's excellent essay: "From Vanity Fair to Emerald City: Baum's Debt to Bunyan," *Children's Literature* 23 (1995): 91–114. See also *The Annotated Wizard of Oz*, ed. Michael Patrick Hearn (New York: W. W. Norton, 2000).

25. As stated in J. Karl Franson, "From Vanity Fair to Emerald City: Baum's Debt to Bunyan," *Children's Literature* 23 (1995): 91–114.

CHAPTER ONE

1. Ola Winslow, *John Bunyan* (New York: The Macmillan Company, 1961), 2.

2. T. B. Macaulay, *The Miscellaneous Writings of Lord Macaulay* (London: 1865), 297.

3. Ibid.

4. David Herbert Donald, *Lincoln* (New York: Simon and Schuster, 1995), 30. "The biblical cadences of Lincoln's later speeches," Donald has written, "owed much to John Bunyan."

CHAPTER TWO

1. A point made powerfully in W. R. Owens, ed., John Bunyan, *The Pilgrim's Progress* (Oxford's World Classics, 2003), xiii.

2. Samuel Rawson Gardiner, *History of England from the Accession of James I to the Outbreak of the Civil War, 1603–1642*, Volume 10 (London: Spottiswoode, 1887), 174.

3. Estelle Ross, *Oliver Cromwell* (New York: Frederick A. Stokes, 1915), 126.

4. John Brown, *John Bunyan: His Life, Times and Work* (London: Wm. Isbister Limited, 1885), 153. See also Christopher Hill, *A Tinker and a Poor Man* (New York: Alfred A. Knopf, 1989), 109.

5. Roger Sharrock, *John Bunyan* (London: Macmillan, 1968), 43.

6. Information provided by the Bedford County Web site: www.bedford.gov.uk/GetResource. aspx?file=Bunyancountygaol.pdf.

7. Sharrock, *John Bunyan*, 43.

8. The account that follows of the network of spies created in the reign of Charles II is taken from John Brown, *John Bunyan: His Life, Times and Work* (London: Wm. Isbister Limited, 1885), 224–25.

9. For the story of Lady Alice Lisle, see pages 339–40 of *The Dictionary of National Biography*, Vol. 33 (London: Macmillan and Co., 1893). There is a serviceable overview of Judge Jeffreys and the Bloody Assizes at: http://en.wikipedia.org/wiki/Bloody_Assizes.

10. See the article "Times Old but Not Good: Judge Jeffreys and His 'Bloody Assize,'" on page 11 of the Wednesday, October 23, 1887, edition of the *New York Times*. It is interesting to note that Jeffreys's crimes against humanity later provided the inspiration for the novel *Captain Blood*.

    For a very detailed account, see pages 429–42 of Thomas Babington Macaulay's *History of England from the Accession of James II*, Vol. 1 (London: Longman, Brown, Green and Longmans, 1849). See also pages 569–70 of Arthur Lyon Cross's *A History of England and Greater Britain* (New York: The Macmillan Company, 1930).

CHAPTER THREE

1. Sharrock, *John Bunyan*, 153.

2. A citation from the Web site: http://en.wikipedia.org/wiki/Harrowden,_Bedfordshire.

3. John Pestell, *Travel with John Bunyan* (Day One Publications, 2002), 9; and also the following Web site:
   http://en.wikipedia.org/wiki/Airship_R101.
4. Brown, *John Bunyan: His Life, Times and Work*, 17–18.
5. Winslow, *John Bunyan*, 10.
6. Sharrock, *John Bunyan*, 11.
7. Winslow, *John Bunyan*, 10.
8. Brown, *John Bunyan: His Life, Times and Work*, 17–18.
9. Ibid., 20.
10. Information gleaned from the following Web site:
    http://www.bedford.gov.uk/Default.aspx/Web/ElstowVillage.
11. Information gleaned from the following Web site:
    http://www.britannica.com/eb/article-9072585/tip-cat.
12. Pestell, *Travel with John Bunyan*, 12.

CHAPTER FOUR

1. Brown, *John Bunyan: His Life, Times and Work*, 96–97.
2. Pestell, *Travel with John Bunyan*, 10.
3. Ibid.
4. Ibid.
5. Information from the biographical essay about Bunyan in the old *Dictionary of National Biography*. See also John Brown, *John Bunyan: His Life, Times and Work* (London: Wm. Isbister Limited, 1885), 36.
6. E. M. Forster, *Marianne Thornton: A Domestic Biography* (London: Edward Arnold Ltd., 1956), 22.
7. Text taken from *Select Biographies: Cromwell and Bunyan*, by Robert Southey, (London: John Murray, 1844), 91. Bunyan himself reports that these incidents took place "when I was but a child [of] nine or ten years old."
8. Brown, *John Bunyan: His Life, Times and Work*, 42.
9. Ibid., 36.
10. Richard L. Greaves, *Glimpses of Glory: John Bunyan and English Dissent* (Stanford, California: Stanford University Press, 2002), 5. Greaves states that Bunyan's parents were not godly. However, Southey's conjecture seems plausible enough to suggest that Margaret Bunyan cared about religion at least enough to make sure her son received a conventional sense of his religious duties.

CHAPTER FIVE

1. Brown, *John Bunyan: His Life, Times and Work*, 34.
2. Southey, in his *Life of Bunyan*, gives the following note with reference to the

trade of a tinker: "Workers in brass, or, in common parlance, tinkers, whose profession bore to that of a brazier the same relation which the cobbler's does to the shoemaker's."

3. *The Dictionary of National Biography* (1886), 275.

4. Greaves, *Glimpses of Glory: John Bunyan and English Dissent*, 4.

5. From the 11th edition of the *Encyclopedia Britannica* (New York: 1910).

6. Brown, *John Bunyan: His Life, Times and Work*, 34.

7. Ibid.

8. Ibid.

9. Ibid., 38.

10. Ibid.

11. Ibid.

12. See page 36 of Brown, *John Bunyan: His Life, Times and Work*.

Chapter Six

1. From an essay on Friedrich Schiller by Thomas Carlyle.

2. The quatrain is from lines 314–17 of William Cowper's poem "Tirocinium."

3. Brown, *John Bunyan: His Life, Times and Work*, 10–11.

4. Ibid., 1.

5. Ibid., 3.

6. Ibid.

7. Ibid.

8. Ibid., 6.

9. Ibid., 7.

10. Winslow, *John Bunyan*, 8.

11. Ibid.

12. Ibid.

13. The information in this paragraph is gleaned from the following Web site: http://vision.edina.ac.uk/text/contents_page.jsp?t_id=Fiennes.

14. Winslow, *John Bunyan*, 9.

15. Ibid., 11.

Chapter Seven

1. From Chapter 33 of *The Life of Samuel Johnson*, by James Boswell.

2. John Bunyan, *Grace Abounding to the Chief of Sinners* (London: Simpkin, Marshall and Co., 1863), 7.

3. Ibid.

4. Ibid.

5. Herbert David Donald, *Lincoln* (New York: Simon & Schuster, 1995), 19.

6. From Thomas Babington, Lord Macaulay's biographical essay on Bunyan, written for the *Encyclopedia Britannica* in May 1854. See T. B. Macaulay, *Critical, Historical and Miscellaneous Essays* (Boston: Gould and Lincoln, 1860), 132.

7. From T. B. Macaulay, *Critical, Historical and Miscellaneous Essays* (Boston: Gould and Lincoln, 1860), 132.

8. Robert Southey, *Select Biographies: Cromwell and Bunyan* (London: John Murray, 1844), 91. In a footnote, the following from Sir Walter Scott's review of Southey's Life of Bunyan in the Quarterly Review (vol. 43, p. 470) is given: "The tinker's trade was not followed, however, by Bunyan's father as an itinerant calling, which leads Mr. Southey to wonder why it should have come to be esteemed so mean. We believe the reason to be that the tinkers' craft is, in Great Britain, commonly practised by gypsies; and we surmise the probability that Bunyan's own family, though reclaimed and settled, might have sprung from this caste of vagabonds: that they were not, at all events, originally English, would seem the most natural explanation of young John's asking his father, whether he was not of Jewish extraction? (expecting thereby to found on the promises made in the Old Testament to the seed of Abraham.)"

9. The descriptor, yeoman, refers to a man who is one of the class of lesser freeholders.

10. Bunyan biographer Edmund Venables takes note of this and observes: "Bunyan seems to be describing his own father and his wandering life when he speaks of "an honest poor labouring man, who, like Adam unparadised, had all the world to get his bread in, and was very careful to maintain his family." See Edmund Venables, *Life of John Bunyan* (London: Walter Scott, 1888), 19.

11. A point made by Bunyan biographer Edmund Venables: "[Thomas Bunyan] and his wife were also careful with a higher care that their children should be properly educated." See Edmund Venables, *Life of John Bunyan* (London: Walter Scott, 1888), 19.

12. From *The Pilgrim's Progress by John Bunyan*, ed. by George W. Latham (Chicago: Scott, Foresman and Company, 1906).

13. Margaret Spufford, *Small Books and Pleasant Histories: Popular Fiction and Its Readership in Seventeenth-Century England* (London: Cambridge University Press, 1985), 49.

14. See the fine article about chapbooks posted on the Web site of the Lily Library at the University of Indiana:
http://www.indiana.edu/~liblilly/chapbook.shtml.

15. Harry Weiss, as quoted from the Web site of the prestigious St. Bride Library, celebrated for its graphic arts collections:
http://stbride.org/events_education/events/oldereventsatthelibrary.

16. The Web site of the Victoria and Albert Museum has an excellent overview of chapbooks and their history, referencing Pepys's collection: http://www.vam.ac.uk/collections/prints_books/Chapbooks/index.html.

17. The Bodleian Library at Oxford University has posted an excellent article, "The Ballads Project," which discusses the prices of chapbooks: http://www.bodley.ox.ac.uk/ballads/project.htm.

18. See the biographical essay on Kirkman in volume 11 of *The Dictionary of National Biography* (New York: Macmillan, 1909). R. C. Bald also published a fine scholarly article about Kirkman, "Francis Kirkman, Bookseller and Author," in *Modern Philology*, University of Chicago Press, Vol. 41, No. 1 (Aug., 1943), 17–32.

19. *Eighteenth-century Popular Culture: A Selection*, ed. John Mullan, Christopher Reid, (Oxford University Press, 2000), 146.

20. Spufford, *Small Books and Pleasant Histories*, 103.

21. Ibid., 111–26.

22. See the biographical essay on pages 327–28 of *The Dictionary of National Biography*, Vol. 14 (London: Macmillan, 1888).

23. See H. V. Routh's review of *The Works of Thomas Deloney* by Francis Oscar Mann in *The Modern Language Review*, Vol. 7, No. 4 (Oct. 1912), 561–64. See also the *Encyclopedia Britannica*'s online article "Prose styles, 1550–1600," at: http://search.eb.com/shakespeare/print?articleId=106051&fullArticle=true&tocId=12816.

24. A point made powerfully by C. S. Lewis and developed further in this book in the pages that follow. See C. S. Lewis, *Selected Essays*, ed. by Walter Hooper (Cambridge University Press, 1969), 147.

25. John Bunyan, *A Few Sighs from Hell* (1658).

26. *The Works of John Bunyan*, ed. George Offor, Vol. 3 (London: Blackie and Son, 1856), 711.

27. For a summary of the legends surrounding St. George, see the definitive historical essay in the *Oxford Dictionary of National Biography*, as posted at the ODNB Web site: http://www.oxforddnb.com/public/dnb/60304.html. See also pages 166–70 of John Ashton, *Chap-books of the Eighteenth Century* (London: Chatto and Windus, 1882); and pages 255–56 of *Christ Lore the Legends, Traditions, Myths, Symbols, Customs and Superstitions of the Christian Church*, by F. W. Hackwood (London: Eliot Stock, 1902). There is also a serviceable summary at: http://en.wikipedia.org/wiki/Saint_George.

28. For a summary of the legends surrounding Bevis of Southampton, see pages 157–63 of John Ashton, *Chap-books of the Eighteenth Century* (London: Chatto and Windus, 1882). The University of Rochester has also posted a concise overview at: http://www.lib.rochester.edu/camelot/teams/bevisint.htm.

29. The background information regarding Bevis of Hampton is gleaned from the following Web site: http://www.lib.rochester.edu/camelot/teams/bevisint.htm.

30. *The Works of John Bunyan*, ed. George Offor, vol. 3 (London: Blackie and Son, 1856), 711.

CHAPTER EIGHT

1. Macaulay's biographical essay on Bunyan was a contribution to the *Encyclopedia Britannica* in May 1854. See volume 3 of *The Miscellaneous Writings of Lord Macaulay*.

2. John Bunyan, *Grace Abounding and The Pilgrim's Progress*, ed. Roger Sharrock (London: Oxford University Press, 1966), 8.

3. Ibid.

4. Ibid.

5. Greaves, *Glimpses of Glory: John Bunyan and English Dissent*, 7.

6. Ibid., 8.

7. John Bunyan, *Grace Abounding and The Pilgrim's Progress*, ed. Roger Sharrock (London: Oxford University Press, 1966), 8.

8. From Thomas Babington Macaulay's biographical essay on Bunyan in the *Encyclopedia Britannica*, submitted in May 1854.

9. John Bunyan, *Grace Abounding and The Pilgrim's Progress*, ed. Roger Sharrock (London: Oxford University Press, 1966), 8–9.

10. Brown, *John Bunyan: His Life, Times and Work*, 42.

11. From "Mortality," by William Knox (1789–1825). A poem remembered today because it was Abraham Lincoln's favorite poem.

12. Brown, *John Bunyan: His Life, Times and Work*, 41.

CHAPTER NINE

1. From Act V, scene 4 of Joseph Addison's play *Cato*.

2. Greaves, *Glimpses of Glory: John Bunyan and English Dissent*, 11.

3. Brown, *John Bunyan: His Life, Times and Work*, 49–50.

4. Greaves, *Glimpses of Glory: John Bunyan and English Dissent*, 11.

5. Ibid., 19.

6. Ibid., 11.

7. Ibid., 12–13.

8. Ibid., 12. See specifically, Luke, *Letter Books*, 22, 25, 27–28, 37, 54, 56, 74, 82, 84, 91, 94–95, 593; BL., Add MS 61,681, fol. 111r; CSPD, 1644–45, 66.9. For the summary of conditions Bunyan and his fellow soldiers faced, described in this and the next several paragraphs, I am indebted to the following source:

Richard Greaves, *Glimpses of Glory: John Bunyan and English Dissent*, (Stanford: Stanford University Press, 2002), 13–15.

9. Ibid.

10. Ibid.

11. Ibid., 15.

12. See Brown, *John Bunyan: His Life, Times and Work*, 322. Here, Brown writes: "If it be true, as has been said, that in *The Pilgrim's Progress* 'Bunyan's men are not merely life portraits but English portraits, men of the solid, practical, unimpassioned Midland race,' it is also true that in *The Holy War* we move in the midst of many of the scenes and surroundings through which Bunyan himself had moved. He may, like Milton, take us down to Pandemonium when Diabolus is in council, or up to the central heaven where the purposes of the Eternal are unfolded; but Mansoul itself, with its walls, gates, strongholds, and sallyport, largely took shape in his mind from the garrison at Newport Pagnell, or the fortifications of the Newarke at Leicester. The army of Shaddai, with its captains clad in armour, its forces marching, counter-marching, opening to the right and to the left, dividing and subdividing, closing, wheeling, making good their front and rear, with their right and left wings, the handling of their arms, the management of their weapons of war . . . all these were reminiscences of Cromwell's army of the new model, and of the military manoeuvres in which he himself had taken part under Sir Samuel Luke."

13. Greaves, *Glimpses of Glory: John Bunyan and English Dissent*, 15.

14. Ibid., 18.

15. John Bunyan, *Grace Abounding and The Pilgrim's Progress*, ed. Roger Sharrock (London: Oxford University Press, 1966), 10.

Chapter Ten

1. From the dedication to Lord Byron's poem *Don Juan*.

2. Greaves, *Glimpses of Glory: John Bunyan and English Dissent*, 30.

3. Ibid.

4. Brown, *John Bunyan: His Life, Times and Work*, 53.

5. Greaves, *Glimpses of Glory: John Bunyan and English Dissent*, 30.

6. Brown, *John Bunyan: His Life, Times and Work*, 54.

7. Ibid., 97.

8. Information provided by the John Bunyan Museum Web site: http://www.bedfordmuseum.org/johnbunyanmuseum/beds.htm.

9. A unit of liquid measure equal to a quarter of a pint.

10. A description of Bunyan from life contained in George Offor's *Memoir of John Bunyan*. See the Preface to *The Works of John Bunyan*, ed. George Offor, vol. 2 (London: Blackie and Son, 1856), vi.

Chapter Eleven

1. John Richard Green, *History of the English People*, vol. 4 (New York: The Useful Knowledge Publishing Company, 1882), 406–07. Here Green writes: "so completely [did] the Bible become Bunyan's life that one feels its phrases as the natural expression of his thoughts. He . . . lived in the Bible till its words [had] become his own."

2. From David McCullough's "The Course of Human Events," the 2003 Jefferson Lecture in the Humanities.

3. C. H. Firth, Cromwell's Army: *A History of the English Solider during the Civil Wars, the Commonwealth and the Protectorate, being the Ford Lectures Delivered in the University of Oxford, 1900–1901* (London: Methuen and Co, Ltd., 1902), 291. Bunyan never served in Cromwell's New Model Army, but this discussion of soldierly sins and their punishments gives an idea of conditions similar to those Bunyan would have witnessed, for he had interaction with soldiers from units that were part of Cromwell's forces. See pages 20–21 of Richard Greaves's *Glimpses of Glory* (Stanford, California: Stanford University Press, 2002).

4. C. H. Firth, Cromwell's Army: *A History of the English Solider during the Civil Wars, the Commonwealth and the Protectorate, being the Ford Lectures Delivered in the University of Oxford, 1900–1901* (London: Methuen and Co, Ltd., 1902), 289.

5. Ibid., 291, 403.

6. Ibid. See in particular the note on the bottom of page 291, which reveals that a number of soldiers were whipped for "illicit amours" with women living in towns near which the soldiers had been posted.

7. Ibid., 290–91.

8. John Bunyan, *Grace Abounding and The Pilgrim's Progress*, ed. Roger Sharrock (London: Oxford University Press, 1966), 10.

9. A line from the Westminster Shorter Catechism, published in 1647, the year of Bunyan's discharge from the army.

Chapter Twelve

1. From G. K. Chesterton's Introduction to John Bunyan, *The Pilgrim's Progress* (London: Cassell and Company, 1904), 11–12.

2. Respectively, Bunyan's Christian and Walton's Piscator.

3. From Andrew Lang's Introduction to *The Compleat Angler*, by Izaak Walton (London: J. D. Dent & Co., 1932), xxii.

4. C. S. Lewis, "Bunyan and *The Pilgrim's Progress*," a BBC radio presentation given on October 16, 1962.

5. John Bunyan, *Grace Abounding*, ed. John Stachniewski, with Anita Pacheco (London: Oxford University Press, 1998).

6. Sharrock, ed., *The Pilgrim's Progress*, xxiv.

7. W. R. Owens, ed., John Bunyan, *The Pilgrim's Progress* (Oxford's World Classics, 2003), lii.

8. Greaves, *Glimpses of Glory: John Bunyan and English Dissent*, 33–34.

9. C. S. Lewis, "Bunyan and *The Pilgrim's Progress*," a BBC radio presentation given on October 16, 1962.

10. Greaves, *Glimpses of Glory: John Bunyan and English Dissent*, 33–34.

11. Ibid., 42.

12. John Bunyan, *Grace Abounding and The Pilgrim's Progress*, ed. Roger Sharrock, (London: Oxford University Press, 1966), 10–11.

13. The identification of the "three inducements" that follows is taken from Greaves, *Glimpses of Glory: John Bunyan and English Dissent*, 33–34.

14. John Bunyan, *Grace Abounding and The Pilgrim's Progress*, ed. Roger Sharrock (London: Oxford University Press, 1966), 11–12.

15. Ibid., 12.

16. Ibid.

17. Ibid., 12–13.

18. Ibid., 13.

19. Ibid.

20. Ecclesiastes 8:15 KJV.

21. John Bunyan, *Grace Abounding and The Pilgrim's Progress*, ed. Roger Sharrock (London: Oxford University Press, 1966), 13.

22. Ibid., 13–14.

23. Ibid., 14–15.

24. Ibid., 16–17.

25. Ibid.

26. Greaves, *Glimpses of Glory: John Bunyan and English Dissent*, 43. See also John Bunyan, *Grace Abounding and The Pilgrim's Progress*, ed. Roger Sharrock, Oxford Standard Authors (London: Oxford University Press, 1966), 17.

CHAPTER THIRTEEN

1. Brown, *John Bunyan: His Life, Times and Work*, 81–82.

2. Ibid., 82. Here, Brown refers the reader to the *Letter from Lord General Fairfax to Speaker Lenthall*, dated Rochester, June 6, 1648; *Newes from Bowe, Rochester*, June 4, 1648; *Narrative of the Great Victory in Kent*; London: Robert Ibbitson in Smithfield, 1648; *Bloody Newes from Kent*, June 1648; *King's Pamphlets*, British Museum.

3. Roughly 30,000 pounds in today's currency.

4. Brown, *John Bunyan: His Life, Times and Work*, 83.

5. Ibid., 94.

6. Ibid.

7. Ibid.

8. John Bunyan, *Grace Abounding and The Pilgrim's Progress*, ed. Roger Sharrock, (London: Oxford University Press, 1966), 68.

9. Ibid., 60.

10. Ibid., 67–68.

11. Greaves, *Glimpses of Glory: John Bunyan and English Dissent*, 34.

12. In the past, tuberculosis was called consumption, because it seemed to consume people from within, with a bloody cough, fever, pallor, and long, relentless wasting.

13. John Bunyan, *Grace Abounding and The Pilgrim's Progress*, ed. Roger Sharrock (London: Oxford University Press, 1966), 81.

14. Ibid., 82.

15. Ibid., 84.

16. Ibid.

17. Ibid.

18. John Bunyan, *The Pilgrim's Progress*, Library of Classics (London & Glasgow: Collins, n.d.), 47–48.

CHAPTER FOURTEEN

1. From Part 2 of Baxter's *Love Breathing Thanks and Praise*.

2. Brown, *John Bunyan: His Life, Times and Work*, 96.

3. Ibid.

4. Ibid., 115.

5. Ibid.

6. Ibid., 120.

7. Ibid.

8. Ibid., 120–21.

9. Charles Doe's account, Folio of 1692.

10. Brown, *John Bunyan: His Life, Times and Work*, 120–22.

11. Ibid., 122–23.

12. The foregoing extended quote and preceding two paragraphs are derived from Brown, *John Bunyan: His Life, Times and Work*, 123–24.

13. Greaves, *Glimpses of Glory: John Bunyan and English Dissent*, 57.

14. Hersen, M., Turner, S. M., and Beidel, D. C. (Eds.). (2007). Adult Psychopathology and Diagnosis (5th ed.). (Hoboken, New Jersey: John Wiley & Sons, Inc.)

15. Brown, *John Bunyan: His Life, Times and Work*, 111. Here, Brown writes: "on the earnest desire of the Church, and after some solemn prayer to the Lord,

with fasting, [Bunyan] was more particularly called forth and appointed to a more ordinary and public preaching of the Word."

16. Ibid., 100.
17. Ibid.
18. Ibid.
19. Sharrock, *John Bunyan*, 49.

Chapter Fifteen

1. A phrase coined by George Offor in his Preface to *The Works of John Bunyan*, Vol. 2, (London: Blackie and Son, 1856), vi.

2. Winslow, *John Bunyan*, 8.

3. The Elstow parish church records contain the following regarding Bunyan's two daughters by his first wife: "Mary, the daughter of John Bonion, was baptized the 20th day of July, 1650." "Elizabeth, the daughter of John Bonyon, was born 14th day of April, 1654." See John Brown, *John Bunyan: His Life, Times and Work* (London: Wm. Isbister Limited, 1885), 96. Bunyan's sons by his first wife, John and Thomas, were likely born between 1654 and 1658.

4. http://en.wikipedia.org/wiki/Richard_Cromwell.

5. See the "Chronology of Bunyan's Life and Times" on page lii of John Bunyan, *The Pilgrim's Progress*, ed. W. R. Owens (Oxford: Oxford University Press, 2003).

6. Greaves, *Glimpses of Glory: John Bunyan and English Dissent*, 142.

7. Brown, *John Bunyan: His Life, Times and Work*, 136.

8. John Bunyan, "A Relation of the Imprisonment . . . ," from page 98 of *Grace Abounding and Other Spiritual Autobiographies*, ed. John Stachniewski, with Anita Pacheco (Oxford: Oxford University Press, 1998).

9. Brown, *John Bunyan: His Life, Times and Work*, 138.

10. John Bunyan, "A Relation of the Imprisonment . . . ," from pages 98–99 of *Grace Abounding and Other Spiritual Autobiographies*, ed. John Stachniewski, with Anita Pacheco (Oxford: Oxford University Press, 1998).

11. The account of Bunyan's arrest that follows is taken from John Brown, *John Bunyan: His Life, Times and Work* (London: Wm. Isbister Limited, 1885), 138.

12. John Bunyan, "A Relation of the Imprisonment . . . ," from page 99 of *Grace Abounding and Other Spiritual Autobiographies*, ed. John Stachniewski, with Anita Pacheco (Oxford: Oxford University Press, 1998).

Chapter Sixteen

1. George Barrell Cheever, *Lectures on The Pilgrim's Progress* (London: A Fullarton and Co., 1846), 4.

2. Greaves, *Glimpses of Glory: John Bunyan and English Dissent*, 133–35.

3. As quoted in Brown, *John Bunyan: His Life, Times and Work*, 152.

4. Greaves, *Glimpses of Glory: John Bunyan and English Dissent*, 135.

5. Brown, *John Bunyan: His Life, Times and Work*, 152.

6. *Judges of England*, by Edward Foss, F.S.A., of the Inner Temple, London, 1870.

7. Brown, *John Bunyan: His Life, Times and Work*, 151.

8. Ibid.

9. Ibid., 153.

10. Greaves, *Glimpses of Glory: John Bunyan and English Dissent*, 137.

11. Brown, *John Bunyan: His Life, Times and Work*, 154.

12. Ibid., 156.

13. Ibid.

14. Ibid., 156–57.

15. John Bunyan, "A Relation of the Imprisonment . . . ," from page 118 of *Grace Abounding and Other Spiritual Autobiographies*, ed. John Stachniewski, with Anita Pacheco (Oxford: Oxford University Press, 1998).

16. Brown, *John Bunyan: His Life, Times and Work*, 157.

17. Ibid., 157–58.

18. Ibid., 158. Here and there, I have made slight changes to the words of the participants in the transcript of this colloquy.

19. Brown, *John Bunyan: His Life, Times and Work*, 158–59. Here and there, I have made slight changes to the words of the participants in the transcript of this colloquy.

20. Brown, *John Bunyan: His Life, Times and Work*, 159.

21. As quoted on page 190 of John Brown, *John Bunyan: His Life, Times and Work*.

22. Ibid.

23. Ibid.

24. The description of the Bedford county gaol that follows is gleaned and at times paraphrased from pages 162–68 of Brown, *John Bunyan: His Life, Times and Work*.

25. John Howard, *State of the Prisons in England and Wales*, Third Edition, 1785, 283.

26. Brown, *John Bunyan: His Life, Times and Work*, 163.

27. Ibid., 167.

28. John Bunyan, *Grace Abounding and The Pilgrim's Progress*, ed. Roger Sharrock (London: Oxford University Press, 1966), 133–34.

29. As quoted in Brown, *John Bunyan: His Life, Times and Work*, 168.

30. Ibid.

31. The provisional date of composition assigned by Greaves in *Glimpses of Glory: John Bunyan and English Dissent*, 637.

32. Brown, *John Bunyan: His Life, Times and Work*, 179.

33. Sharrock, *John Bunyan*, 43.

34. The description of the Bedford county gaol given above is gleaned and at times paraphrased from pages 162–68 of John Brown, *John Bunyan: His Life, Times and Work* (London: Wm. Isbister Limited, 1885).

35. John Bunyan, *Grace Abounding and The Pilgrim's Progress*, ed. Roger Sharrock, Oxford Standard Authors (London: Oxford University Press, 1966), 100. I have slightly changed the wording here for the sake of clarity.

Chapter Seventeen

1. From volume 1 of *The Miscellaneous Writings of Lord Macaulay*.

2. See the footnote on page 118 of Brown, *John Bunyan: His Life, Times and Work*.

3. Brown, *John Bunyan: His Life, Times and Work*, 118–19.

4. A chronology given on page xxv of Roger Sharrock's edition of *The Pilgrim's Progress* (London: Penguin Classics, 1987).

5. C. S. Lewis, "The Vision of John Bunyan," in *Selected Literary Essays* (1969), 147.

6. John Richard Green, History of the English People, vol. 4, (New York: 1882), 406–07.

7. Cheever, *Lectures on The Pilgrim's Progress*, 9.

8. C. S. Lewis, "The Vision of John Bunyan," in *Selected Literary Essays* (1969), 147–48.

Chapter Eighteen

1. Brown, *John Bunyan: His Life, Times and Work*, 262.

2. From G. K. Chesterton's Introduction to John Bunyan, *The Pilgrim's Progress* (London: Cassell and Company, 1904), 11–12.

3. John Bunyan, *Grace Abounding and The Pilgrim's Progress*, ed. Roger Sharrock (London: Oxford University Press, 1966), 146.

4. From Perry Keenlyside's introductory essay for the Naxos Audio Book edition of *The Pilgrim's Progress* (1999).

5. J. W. Cross, ed., *George Eliot's Life, as Related in Her Letters and Journals*, vol. 2 (Boston: Estes and Lauriat, 1895), 110.

6. Brown, *John Bunyan: His Life, Times and Work*, 253.

7. See the timeline on page xxv of Roger Sharrock's edition of *The Pilgrim's Progress* (London: Penguin Classics, 1987). See also page 210 of Greaves, *Glimpses of Glory: John Bunyan and English Dissent*. Here, Greaves writes that Bunyan began writing *The Pilgrim's Progress* in March 1668, or about a year later than Sharrock believes Bunyan began writing. Lastly, see page liv of W. R. Owens, ed., John Bunyan, *The Pilgrim's Progress* (Oxford's World Classics,

2003). Here, W. R. Owens states that Bunyan was released from his first imprisonment in March 1772.

8. Greaves, *Glimpses of Glory: John Bunyan and English Dissent*, 220.

9. Ibid., 342.

10. Sharrock, *John Bunyan*, 49. See also the Web site of the John Bunyan Museum:

http://www.bedfordmuseum.org/johnbunyanmuseum/beds.htm.

11. Sharrock, *John Bunyan*, 70.

12. Greaves, *Glimpses of Glory: John Bunyan and English Dissent*, 344.

13. Sharrock, *John Bunyan*, 49.

14. Greaves, *Glimpses of Glory: John Bunyan and English Dissent*, 344.

15. Greaves, *Glimpses of Glory: John Bunyan and English Dissent*, 342.

16. In the paragraphs that follow, I have presented a slightly paraphrased version of Brown's summary of the plot of *The Pilgrim's Progress*, which appears on pages 267–72 of John Brown, *John Bunyan: His Life, Times and Work* (London: Wm. Isbister Limited, 1885).

17. Once again, in the paragraphs above, I have presented a slightly paraphrased version of Brown's summary of the plot of *The Pilgrim's Progress*, which appears on pages 267–72 of John Brown, *John Bunyan: His Life, Times and Work* (London: Wm. Isbister Limited, 1885).

18. John Bunyan, *Grace Abounding and The Pilgrim's Progress*, ed. Roger Sharrock (Oxford University Press, 1966), 187–88.

19. Once again, in the paragraphs below, I have presented a slightly paraphrased version of Brown's summary of the plot of *The Pilgrim's Progress*, which appears on pages 267–72 of Brown, *John Bunyan: His Life, Times and Work*.

20. John Bunyan, *Grace Abounding and The Pilgrim's Progress*, ed. Roger Sharrock (London: Oxford University Press, 1966), 210.

21. Brown, *John Bunyan: His Life, Times and Work*, 270.

CHAPTER NINETEEN

1. A description of *The Pilgrim's Progress* from Roosevelt's speech at the Minnesota State Fair, Minneapolis, Sept. 2, 1902.

2. Gary Scott Smith, *Faith and the Presidency: From George Washington to George W. Bush* (Oxford: Oxford University Press, 2006), 156. This is a partial citation of Roosevelt's speech at the Minnesota State Fair, Minneapolis, Sept. 2, 1902.

3. Brown, *John Bunyan: His Life, Times and Work*, 266, 272.

4. Ibid., 273.

5. Ibid.

6. Ibid.

7. Ibid.

8. Ibid.

9. Ibid.

10. I am indebted to John Brown for his summary and observations concerning the plot for the Second Part of *The Pilgrim's Progress*. See Brown, *John Bunyan: His Life, Times and Work*, 276–81.

11. Brown, *John Bunyan: His Life, Times and Work*, 278.

12. Ibid., 279.

13. Ibid.

14. Ibid., 281.

CHAPTER TWENTY

1. Cheever, *Lectures on The Pilgrim's Progress*, 1.

2. Brown, *John Bunyan: His Life, Times and Work*, 305.

3. The first American edition of *The Pilgrim's Progress* was published by Samuel Green of Boston in 1681.

4. Sharrock, *John Bunyan*, 49.

5. Robert Southey, ed., *The Pilgrim's Progress, with a Life of John Bunyan* (New York: Harper and Brothers, 1837), 55–56. See also page 382 of Brown, *John Bunyan: His Life, Times and Work*. This story may be apocryphal. The classic and authoritative 1911 edition of the *Encyclopedia Britannica* reports that Owen "ardently admired" Bunyan's preaching and worked hard to secure Bunyan's release from his second imprisonment. It does not, however, mention the story involving Charles II. See page 393 of the *Encyclopedia Britannica*, vol 20 (Cambridge: Cambridge University Press, 1911).

6. Sharrock, *John Bunyan*, 49.

7. Ibid.

8. Brown, *John Bunyan: His Life, Times and Work*, 350.

9. Sharrock, *John Bunyan*, 49–50. See also pages 358–59 of Brown, *John Bunyan* (1885): "there was . . . a strangely altered world in England . . . Bunyan's local influence with the Nonconformists made him of sufficient importance to be sought after in the service of the Government . . . 'a great man in those days, coming to Bedford . . . sent for [Mr. Bunyan] to give him a place of public trust, [but he] would by no means come [and] sent his excuse.' This great man . . . was [the] Earl of Ailesbury [sic] . . .

"To understand Bunyan's position . . . it is necessary to [know] the general history of the time. The King, a Roman Catholic . . . resolved to give his own religion an equal standing in the country with [the Church of England] . . . Authority was granted to avowed Romanists among the clergy to remain in their livings; bishoprics as they fell vacant were filled up by sycophants on whom he could rely; and the Court of High Commission, after being long laid aside, was once more set up and invested with absolute control over universities, colleges, cathedrals, and all ecclesiastical corporations whatever, with power of summary excommunication and deprivation of all and sundry who might be disobedient.

"The result . . . was soon manifest . . . convents rose and eminent converts were made; the Franciscans found a home in Lincoln's Inn Fields, the Carmelites in the city, the Benedictines at St. James's Palace, and the Jesuits in the Savoy. Bad feeling sprang up between contending [religious] parties, and street riots resulted. A mass-house was broken into in Cheapside, the crucifix carried out and fixed on the parish-pump, and when [soldiers] were called out to put down the riot, they flatly refused to fight in favour of popery.

"The King . . . now rapidly estranging his former friends, sought by a deep stroke of policy to win the Nonconformists to his side . . . he proceeded to annul a long series of statutes, and suspended all penal laws against all classes of Nonconformists. [He] also dispensed with all religious tests. Constitutionalists and Churchmen grew alarmed, and now they on their part tried to win the Nonconformists over to their side. Thus began what has been called *the strangest auction* recorded in history, when the Protestant Dissenters, who had lately been the religious outcasts of the country, held the balance of power between the King and the Church [of England]."

10. George Offer, ed. *The Whole Works of John Bunyan*, vol. 2 (London: Blackie and Son, 1862), 694.

11. Ibid., 709.

Chapter Twenty-One

1. James Anthony Froude, *John Bunyan* (New York: Harper and Brothers, 1880), 171.

2. Brown, *John Bunyan: His Life, Times and Work*, 386–87.

3. See page xxx of Edmund Venables's biographical introduction to John Bunyan, *Pilgrim's Progress, Grace Abounding and A Relation of His Imprisonment*, Second Edition, revised by Mabel Peacock (Oxford: Clarendon Press, 1900).

4. Greaves, *Glimpses of Glory: John Bunyan and English Dissent*, 599.

5. Ibid., 598.

6. Brown, *John Bunyan: His Life, Times and Work*, 390.

7. Ibid.

8. Ibid.

EPILOGUE

1. http://www.bedfordmuseum.org/johnbunyanmuseum/background1.htm.
2. A phrase from John Cheke, as quoted in Simon Winchester, *The Meaning of Everything: The Story of the Oxford English Dictionary* (New York: HarperCollins, 2003), 7.

SELECT BIBLIOGRAPHY

Brown, John, *John Bunyan: His Life, Times and Work* (London: Wm. Isbister Ltd, 1885).

Bunyan, John, *Grace Abounding to the Chief of Sinners and The Pilgrim's Progress*, ed. Roger Sharrock, Oxford Standard Authors Series (London: Oxford University Press, 1966).

————, *Grace Abounding, with Other Spiritual Biographies*, ed. John Stachniewski and Anita Pacheco (Oxford: Oxford World's Classics, 1998).

————, *The Life and Death of Mr. Badman*, foreword by James Fenton (London: Hesperus Classics, 2007).

————, *The Pilgrim's Progress*, ed. Roger Sharrock (London: Penguin Books, 1965).

————, *The Pilgrim's Progress*, rev. ed. Roger Sharrock (London: Penguin Books, 1987).

————, *The Pilgrim's Progress*, ed. W. R. Owens (Oxford: Oxford's World Classics, 2003).

————, *The Pilgrim's Progress*, ed. Roger Pooley (London: Penguin Classics, 2009).

————, *The Pilgrim's Progress, Illustrated by Nearly Three Hundred Engravings* (London: Samuel Bagster and Sons., 1845).

————, *The Works of John Bunyan*, ed. George Offor, 3 vols., (London: W. G. Blackie and Son, 1856).

Bush, Douglas, *English Literature in the Earlier Seventeenth Century* (Oxford: Clarendon Press, 1945).

Cheever, George Barrell, *Lectures on The Pilgrim's Progress* (New York: Robert Carter & Brothers, 1853).

Davies, Michael, *Graceful Reading: Theology and Narrative in the Works of John Bunyan* (Oxford: Oxford University Press, 2002).

Froude, James Anthony, *Bunyan*, English Men of Letters Series (New York: Harper & Brothers, Publishers, 1880).

Greaves, Richard, *Glimpses of Glory: John Bunyan and English Dissent* (Stanford: Stanford University Press, 2002).

Hill, Christopher, *A Tinker and a Poor Man* (New York: Knopf, 1989).

Lewis, C. S., *The Literary Impact of the Authorized Version* (Philadelphia: Fortress Press, 1963).

Lewis, C. S., *Selected Essays*, ed. by Walter Hooper (Cambridge: Cambridge University Press, 1969).

Macaulay, Thomas Babington, *Critical and Historical Essays*, vol. 2 (London: J. M. Dent & Sons, 1919).

Southey, Robert, *Select Biographies: Cromwell and Bunyan* (London: John Murray, 1844).

Winslow, Ola, *John Bunyan* (New York: Macmillan, 1968).

ACKNOWLEDGMENTS

I should like to begin by thanking David McCullough for his many eloquent reflections about the influence of *The Pilgrim's Progress* on America's greatest leaders and her citizens more generally. His thoughts on how Bunyan's masterwork touched the lives of presidents Truman, Roosevelt, and Adams provided me with the initial inspiration for this book. I am in his debt.

Throughout the process of creating this book, Bucky Rosenbaum has been a treasured mentor and friend. I feel a great debt of gratitude for the counsel and advocacy he has provided as my literary agent. No author could have been better served than I have been.

I am deeply grateful as well to Joel Miller, Kristen Parrish, Heather Skelton, and their associates at Thomas Nelson, my publisher. Joel tendered the invitation to contribute to the Christian Encounter series—and has demonstrated on many occasions his commitment to this book and others in development. His vision for this series has been an inspiration. To this I would add that the contributions of Kristen, Heather, and their colleagues on the editorial and design teams at Thomas Nelson have been invaluable. My sincere thanks to one and all.

Aside from my colleagues at Thomas Nelson, I have been fortunate indeed in the friendships that have grown out of my literary travels, and my research over the last several years has taken me to England many times. On several occasions, Lady Davson has welcomed me (and my family) to her lovely home in that most storied of literary places, Mermaid Street in Rye. Thank you, Kate, for so many things.

Sam and Sarah Wilberforce opened their beautiful home in Dorset to my wife, Kelly, and me. And it was there that they both voiced an early enthusiasm for the idea of this book that prompted me to write. I shall always be grateful for conversations with them by the fire, and walks in country fields or along the shore in Lyme Regis. I thank them for the gift of their friendship, as I do the other members of the Wilberforce family who have accorded me the honor of theirs.

John Julius, Lord Norwich, has been a valued friend for several years. He has shown me (and my books) many kindnesses, and I am very grateful that he took time to read this book while it was in manuscript and offer his reflections—even as he was in the midst of readying his own memoirs for the press. I count it a privilege to have heard him speak on the lessons of history at Syon House, and reflect more broadly on life and literature during a train trip we took together to Hull.

With great fondness, I remember many visits to Brian Edwards's home in Surbiton—where I have been treated to fine meals, countryside walks, and sojourns in his garden. His wise counsel and early encouragement of this book has meant a great deal to me.

Canon David Isherwood has shown me many marks of

kindness, as has his wife, Anne, and the parishioners of Holy Trinity Church, Clapham. I would also like to thank Jonathan and Hazel Shaw, and the community at St. Paul's Church, Mill Hill, for their gifts of hospitality and thoughtfulness. I shall long remember an early morning walk while in Mill Hill to Dr. James Murray's scriptorium—with its hallowed connections to the Oxford English Dictionary.

For many years, Os Guinness has been a valued mentor and friend. His early enthusiasm for this book was a catalyst for which I am very grateful.

Early on, Phil Cooke read the first few chapters I had written. He provided me with what so many authors need *in medias res*— the gift of seven words: "I can't wait to get the book." For kindred encouragement, friendship, and advice, I am grateful to Chris Underation. And in countless ways, Ken and Judy Hayes have reminded me anew of the many gifts friendship can bestow.

Brian Sibley generously sent me a personally inscribed set of his masterful dramatization of *The Pilgrim's Progress*, which he posted shortly after we met in London when we were both being interviewed by the BBC. My wife, Kelly, and I treasure this adaptation—not only for its richness but for the mark of friendship and kindness it represents.

Lastly, I would like to thank my wife, Kelly, and my son, Sam—with whom I have shared the gift of days and months and years. I haven't the words to say how much you mean to me; but I can at least tell you how grateful I am for allowing me the time to write this book.

ABOUT THE AUTHOR

Kevin Belmonte holds a B.A. in English Literature from Gordon College, an M.A. in Church History from Gordon-Conwell Seminary, and a second master's degree in American and New England Studies from the University of Southern Maine (Portland).

His first biography, *William Wilberforce: A Hero for Humanity* (Zondervan/HarperCollins, 2007) is now in its fourth printing in paperback. Portions of his Wilberforce biography were taught as part of a course on leadership and character formation at the Kennedy School of Government at Harvard, by professor and CNN political commentator David Gergen, who serves as the director of the KSG's Center for Public Leadership.

Following the publication of *A Hero for Humanity*, Belmonte received the prestigious John Pollock Award for Christian Biography. For six years, he served as the lead historical consultant for the major motion picture *Amazing Grace*.

He has written for many periodicals, including *Christian History* and *Christianity Today*. He and his wife, Kelly, are the proud parents of a four-year-old son, Sam.

The **CHRISTIAN ENCOUNTERS** series

JOHANN SEBASTIAN BACH
RICK MARSCHALL

WILLIAM F. BUCKLEY
JEREMY LOTT

Coming August 2010

ST. FRANCIS
ROBERT WEST

ANNE BRADSTREET
D.B. KELLOGG

J.R.R. TOLKIEN
MARK HORNE

THOMAS NELSON
Since 1798